Before You Go Abroad

Handbook

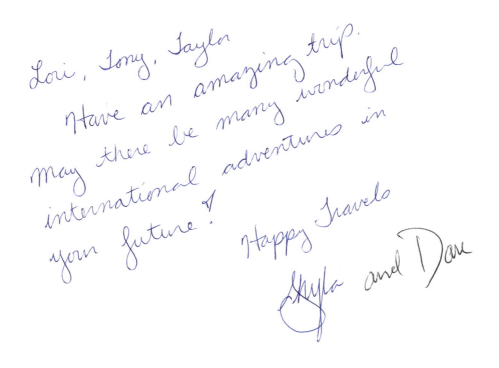

Lori, Tony, Taylor
Have an amazing trip.
May there be many wonderful
international adventures in
your future!
Happy Travels
Skyla and Dave

Travel Smart Strategies

Before You Go Abroad Handbook

Over 127 Secret Tips & Tools

for International Travel

Shyla Esko Bare

Daniel Bare

Wild Spirit Travel, LLC

www.WildSpiritTravel.com

Published by Wild Spirit Travel, LLC, www.WildSpiritTravel.com

Edited by Kari Filburn, Line by Line Copyediting, www.LBLedit.com
Cover design by Daniel Bare
Cover photo compliments of Rawpixel.com via Unsplash.com
Clipart from OpenClipArt.org
Printed in the United States of America

ISBN – 978-1537322346

Dedicated to Xandra Esko

Many travelers ask someone to water plants or feed a pet when on a trip. Dan and I asked my sister, Xandra, to deal with anything and everything that came up stateside. Not a big deal when we thought we would be overseas for six months. However, when we returned to the States after living and traveling abroad for twelve years, we owed Xandra a huge thank you. Here it is, Sis-a-roo: *Thank you for all you did for us while we traveled abroad. Your help was invaluable, as many times you went over and above the call of duty. We may not have always shown our appreciation, but we always felt it. Thanks!*

Praise for Wild Spirit Travel's Before You Go Abroad class

"Before You Go is an absolute MUST for anyone planning to travel overseas. It was outstanding. So many valuable travel tips. I have lived and traveled abroad for 14 years, so I feel that I'm an experienced traveler. That said, I learned lots of useful information."

~ Roger, Tacoma, 2016

"Wow! So much info that I never would have thought to ask."

~ Annette, Vancouver, 2017

"This class increased my travel enthusiasm, as I learned from real world travelers. Good information on how to deal with money, travel health, and more. Loved the useable travel planning checklist."

~ Roberta, Bellevue, 2015

"So much great information! Well organized, I learned a ton, and I feel more confident."

~ Nancy, Portland, 2016

"Very comprehensive on resources available to make travel and accommodation decisions. Quite the exceptional class, which was clearly well worth my time and the cost. Highly recommend. Thanks to both Shyla and Dan!"

~ Matthew, Vancouver, 2017

See numerous reviews for Wild Spirit Travel classes, from real travelers like you, on our website at www.wildspirittravel.com.

Table of Contents

Table of Contents

Preface

I still remember sitting on the floor in my parent's living room, idly watching a travel program on television. Someone on the show mentioned an organization for people who had visited over one hundred countries—the Travelers' Century Club. In that moment, my life changed because I knew that was my destiny. I was fifteen, and even though I had only been to Canada, I knew.

That is why when I met Dan, one of the important factors in determining if we were compatible was how much he traveled. Dan was an active business traveler, normally flying to a client site every week. That was a good sign, and when we decided to get married, I suggested our honeymoon be a trip around the world. This was a big jump for both of us since at that time I had only added Australia and Japan to my list of countries and Dan had only been to a few international destinations as well. Still, we decided to explore the dream, and I started researching.

I read numerous travel memoirs and studied country guidebooks. We met with friends who had gone on extended international trips. I filled notebooks with ideas—but the more I researched, the more questions I had. I was starting to think the idea of traveling around the world was too daunting, then Dan was offered a six-month contract job in Scotland. We jumped at the opportunity to not just travel, but to live abroad.

Within weeks, we moved to Edinburgh—where six months turned into five years. In that time, we traveled extensively around the United Kingdom and Europe. But we had yet to take our *honeymoon*—our long-dreamed-about trip around the world.

It took all of our courage—and a dash of insanity according to our families—but Dan and I finally decided to quit our jobs, sell our stuff, and travel for a year. During our time in Scotland, I had continued to research how to travel internationally, compiling loads of notes. Some of the information was useful, some overwhelming—and we still had questions.

I recall my excitement when I met a woman in Scotland who had done a trip around the world. I asked her question after question—I desperately wanted to talk to someone who had *been there, done that*. Her most profound piece of advice was that Dan and I would be nervous about every country before going there, but after a few days we would feel comfortable. Then, we would not want to leave, since we would be nervous about the next country. It sounded crazy, but after embarking on our trip around the world, we discovered it was accurate.

Even now that Dan and I are seasoned travelers, who have been to over seventy countries on six continents, we still get nervous about a new destination. However, we have amassed numerous tips and tools that reduce the anxiety and prepare us for international travel, so we can enjoy a new country from day one. And enjoying oneself is really what travel is about.

That is why when Dan and I returned to the United States after traveling the world—for not the planned one year but an extended seven years—we founded Wild Spirit Travel. Our goal is to share with travelers the secrets we wished we had known *before* we started traveling. We have created twenty travel classes that we teach at colleges, libraries, clubs, and other venues. Some are also available digitally (www.wildspirittravel.com/courses).

Before You Go Abroad Handbook: Over 127 Secret Tips and Tools for International Travel is our first book and is based on our International Travel Prep: Before You Go Abroad class. It is loaded with resources and insights for traveling internationally. Many of these secrets we had to learn the hard way while traveling. Although Dan and I wrote this book together, the narration is from my perspective to make it easier to follow. You will also see slight variations in some of our tips, based on our personal preferences.

Whether you are planning a two-week holiday to Europe, an eight-week sojourn to Central America, a six-month trip through Southeast Asia or—as we once were—a yearlong trip around the world, this book will give you valuable information to help you prepare for your travels.

~ Shyla Esko Bare

Acknowledgments

Pam and Kevin Jeffery, our first friends who traveled around the world, we thank you for showing us it could be done. We really did enjoy looking through *all* your photos, honest.

We also enjoyed hearing travel stories from Jenny Schoonbee and Mark McClure, who gave us a realistic description of what long-distance bus journeys are like in developing countries. Without your insights, we may not have survived our first eight-hour bus ride with chickens, no air-conditioning, and no bathroom stop.

We are very appreciative of my parents, Maurice and Theldona Esko, for cheering us on and actually having a map on their wall for seven years, tracking our adventures.

For encouraging us to follow our business dreams with Wild Spirit Travel, we thank Ronnie Noize of DIY Marketing Center.

And for helping us transform our rough draft into a useful travel handbook, we are grateful to Kari Filburn of Line by Line Copyediting.

Chapter One

Planning Your International Trip

Planning is an important first step for your international travels, but how much planning should you do? Is it better to have a detailed itinerary or nothing more than a one-way ticket? The answer depends on many factors that are discussed in this chapter.

Even if you think you will just travel on a wing and a prayer, you at least need to decide on your first destination. So, everyone must do some planning. As such, this chapter is applicable to every traveler. For those who like to strategize and research, the planning stage can be an enjoyable part of the trip. Reading guidebooks, dreaming of destinations, and talking to other travelers are ways to not only gather information but to also be inspired about traveling.

Planning Ahead versus Winging It

There are two main approaches to preparing for an international trip: planning ahead and winging it. Which way is best completely depends on the person, the destination, the length of the trip, and a host of other factors. There is no right way on this; however, it may be best to include a little of both into a trip.

Planning Ahead

It works best to plan ahead when time is limited. If you have a one- or two-week vacation, it makes sense to have most things booked so you are not spending all of your holiday trying to find the next place to stay. On short trips, it may make sense to do a tour, but find one that matches your travel style. Dan and I like to get off the beaten path and look for customizable tours or ones that offer a lot of free time. Sometimes it is nice to have someone else coordinate transportation, but we still want the opportunity to take in the foreign culture on our own. That way we get serendipitous travel adventures that are unique for us, even if on a tour.

If not on a tour, we recommend at least planning your first night in a country. After a long international flight, it is nice to know that you have somewhere to go when you arrive. This is especially true if arriving at night. We don't do this every time, in every country, but we do it more often than not and strongly recommend it for anyone new to international travel.

If Dan and I don't have our first night reserved, we still try to research what part of town we would like to stay in, with the name and address for at least one feasible accommodation option. This is useful for completing country entry documents, since almost every country asks for a local address on the immigration entry form. If you don't have a name and address of a hotel, then your entry can be delayed. It is always best to have at least one place in mind when you enter a country.

We also like to have the last night of the trip planned. We usually arrive in the departure city the day before our international flight home to allow time for any what-if situations. If it's an early-morning flight, we stay near the airport. Otherwise, we often splurge on the last night so we return from our vacation nice and rested.

We recommend planning ahead if traveling during peak times. For many countries, this means their summer, especially if there are long school holidays then. In Europe, this is July and August. On the other hand, in Australia, New Zealand, and South America, this is December and January. Dan and I went to Argentina one December. Once there, we decided to go south to the Patagonia region. When we tried to find transport, we discovered the buses were booked out for weeks. The locals were on holiday, and they, too, were headed south, so we had to rethink what we did in Argentina. That was fine, as we did not have our hearts set on any one thing, but if you do, then make sure you can get to what you want to see or do.

For instance, many people going to France have their hearts set on going up the Eiffel Tower in Paris. They sell tickets online beginning ninety days out, and these do sell out. If you have a must do on your trip, plan ahead.

It's also good to plan ahead when traveling outside of your comfort zone, such as to a country where you do not speak the language or one that is known to be difficult (e.g., poor infrastructure, high crime rates). In these cases, it makes sense to have some plans in place. We had reservations for our first week in China and Kenya.

Winging It

Sometimes it is enjoyable to travel without an agenda. No checklist of sights to see, simply an open mind to do whatever strikes your fancy each day. Basking in serendipitous encounters and unusual experiences can create the best travel memories. However, arriving in a foreign land without a set itinerary may feel daunting. Don't let the fear drive you to plot out everything. Dan and I learned that the anxiety subsides after a few days in a new country, then it becomes easier and enjoyable to wing it.

Having flexibility in your travels so you can take the advice of locals or other travelers is perhaps the best thing about winging it. On one trip, Dan and I had around-the-world flights that allowed *open jaws* (meaning we could fly into one location and out from another). We capitalized on this by flying into Kenya and out of Tanzania. The flights were two months apart and, besides our first week in Nairobi, we had nothing else planned. We decided to wing it and find the wonders of the region as we went. This flexibility meant we were able to attend a wedding when locals we met invited us. It was a fun way to see true Kenyan life, something we would not have experienced if we planned everything from home.

We regularly ask locals what they suggest we do. We like to know what someone from *that* place thinks are the best things to do, which often is an activity or place that is not listed in a guidebook. So, if you don't need to, don't overplan. Give yourself free time in your trip itinerary to discover great activities as you go.

A final consideration on when to wing it is if you are going to a country you consider easy (e.g., a place where you speak the language, the tourist infrastructure is strong, there is a high safety rating). Returning to a familiar destination can also make things easier. When these things are in place, consider planning only a few days at the start and end of your trip, with lots of free time in between to wander and explore.

Travel Planning Checklist

No matter your destination, there is some planning that needs to be done. It may simply be buying your plane ticket. Or you may need to apply for tourist visas, stop your mail, buy the right travel gear, get various inoculations, and more.

Not entirely sure what you need to do before traveling abroad? No worries, we have created the Wild Spirit Travel's Travel Planning Checklist (www.wildspirittravel.com/book-checklist) to aid you. It helps with scheduling tasks and lists things for you to do all the way from a year before your trip to the night before. Not every activity will apply to every traveler: it will depend on how long you are traveling for and how much planning you like to do. Use the checklist as a guide to getting your ducks in a row before you go. And remember, the goal of the list is to prepare you to leave home with confidence, knowing that all is fine at home while you are away having an amazing trip.

When to Go Abroad

Dan and I can provide lots of advice on how to travel, but we can't tell you where to go—there are just so many options around the world. But whatever place is calling to you, you should do some research on the best time to visit.

You're Getting Hotter

Weather is important. Destinations can get freezing cold or boiling hot, while some places have torrential rains. A good resource to check on weather for every country is the World Reviewer Holiday Weather Guide (www.worldreviewer.com/world-weather). The site has a world map that changes based on the month and temperature range you select. Orange places on the map are classified as too hot, blue is too cold, while dark green is too wet. Using this map, you can be like Goldilocks and find the destinations that are just right for you to travel to. This website gives temperatures in Celsius (C). To convert Celsius to Fahrenheit (F), or vice versa, use the Calculator Site (www.thecalculatorsite.com/conversions/temperature).

Sometimes, you will never find ideal weather. According to World Reviewer, Scotland is permanently a blue country for me, meaning always too cold. Sure, if you go there you will probably need a coat, even in summer since the average high in August is only 18°C or 64°F. But that is as warm as it gets, so don't just rule it out because it is classified as cold. Just know in advance to pack a fleece or two.

Shoulder Seasons

It can be nice to visit places in their shoulder season, which is the time on either side of their peak season. For Europe, peak season is summer—June through August. That makes spring and autumn the shoulder seasons.

Usually a traveler will find shoulder seasons to be less crowded but still an enjoyable time to visit. Be aware, though, not all tourist attractions are open in shoulder seasons or they may have shorter hours. Dan and I prefer to travel in shoulder seasons to avoid crowds. Plus, it can be a real money saver, since accommodations can be found for a fraction of what is charged in peak season.

Just exactly when is shoulder season? This depends on three factors: weather, when the locals have vacation, and when the main tourist base has vacation. For instance, the best weather in Thailand is November through January, so this is a high travel time. But since many tourists come from Europe and the United States, where vacations are often taken June through August, this can also be a busy season. That means shoulder months for Thailand are February (after the best weather but before it is sweltering hot) and

October (after the foreign travelers have left and before the best weather draws people again). Want to know when other shoulder seasons are? Check out the article "Shoulder Seasons Around the World" by Jennifer V. Cole, on the Travel+Leisure website (www.travelandleisure.com/articles/shoulder-seasons).

Happy Holidays

Before you go abroad, also consider the local holidays. In the United States, there are nine national holidays: New Year's Day, Martin Luther King Day, Presidents' Day, Memorial Day, Independence Day, Labor Day, Veterans Day, Thanksgiving Day, and Christmas Day. Some holidays do not impact international travelers, except that banks are closed. Others have a big impact, such as Thanksgiving weekend, which are the busiest air travel days in the United States. A foreigner here at the end of November may be surprised to not find any flights available since this is not a holiday they have.

Check the local holidays for the destinations you plan to visit to avoid unexpected problems. Dan and I found ourselves stuck in Kuala Lumpur, Malaysia, when we arrived just before Hari Raya Puasa. We had flown to Malaysia from Cambodia and had plans to spend a couple days in Kuala Lumpur before heading north through Malaysia then eventually into Thailand. We had not done our research and had no idea Ramadan was going on. We also did not know that when Ramadan ends, there is a holiday in Malaysia called Hari Raya Puasa. For it, many people return home for large family feasts. As such, transport around the country was busy with locals traveling home. We arrived in Kuala Lumpur ignorant of all of this, and then discovered we could not get a bus or train onward since everything was fully booked for days.

The need to research local holidays was a lesson we learned the hard way. Dan and I now recommend you find out what is going on before you go abroad. A helpful resource is the "Holidays and Observances around the World" page on the Time and Date website (www.timeanddate.com/holidays).

Safety First

It is also wise to research the safety of the location you want to travel to. A useful resource is the US Department of State website (travel.state.gov). On the home page, find the "Learn about Your Destination" section and the box immediately below it. Type the country you are traveling to in the box, and click Go.

On country pages, you will find a box on the right labeled "Assistance for U.S. Citizens," which includes embassy and consular information. If there are any current concerns, they will be listed under the country flag on the left as an alert or warning. Below that, there are quick facts with important information for tourists. Then there is a list of topics with in-depth information. One topic covered for every country is "Safety and Security."

Sometimes the government warnings are overly cautious, deal with weather, or only refer to a specific area of the country. An example is the yearly alert in some regions that warns travelers of hurricane and typhoon season. Do read the details to understand what the real safety and security concerns are and if they impact places you want to travel to. You may be able to happily vacation in a country simply by avoiding the trouble areas.

Smart Traveler Enrollment Program

There is a free program, for American citizens, through the US government where you can enroll your trips abroad with the nearest embassy or consulate. This is advisable if traveling long term, to remote destinations, or to areas with safety concerns. It is called Smart Traveler Enrollment Program (STEP). Having the local embassy know you are in country is useful if there is an emergency situation, such as the 2015 earthquake in Nepal. To enroll, go to the US Department of State STEP website (step.state.gov).

Get a Second Opinion

For a second opinion, on the safety of a destination, Dan and I go to the United Kingdom (UK) "Foreign Travel Advice" page (www.gov.uk/foreign-travel-advice). At the time this book was written, the "Safety and Security" section on Central African Republic begins with, "There are reports of rebel activities, banditry and hostage-taking across the country."[1] Well, that is enough to keep us from vacationing there.

---

1. "Foreign Travel Advice Central African Republic—Safety and Security," GOV.UK, accessed May 23, 2017, www.gov.uk/foreign-travel-advice/central-african-republic/safety-and-security.

For Mexico it says, "Drug-related violence in Mexico has increased over recent years. The violence is concentrated in specific areas, and some regions are almost completely spared."[2] Based on that, Dan and I did our research and traveled to what are considered safe areas, where we had a lovely time. The UK website also has a map for many countries on its website, so you can easily see the areas with safety or security issues.

Location Research Tools

Once you have decided where to go and have checked out the weather, local holidays, and safety situation, it's time to start some in-depth research. This includes discovering what wondrous things there are to see and do at the location, what delicious foods you must try while there, and more. Here are some tools Dan and I use for in-depth destination research.

Guidebooks

Guidebooks can be a good starting point, and there are lots to choose from. The following companies publish informative guidebook series

- DK Eyewitness Travel
- Fodor's Travel
- Footprint Travel Guides
- Frommer's
- Lonely Planet
- National Geographic
- Rick Steves' Guidebooks
- Rough Guides

---

2. "Foreign Travel Advice Mexico—Safety and Security," GOV.UK, accessed June 1, 2017, www.gov.uk/foreign-travel-advice/mexico/safety-and-security.

These are just the ones Dan and I have used. There are more. With so many options, it can be hard to choose. They provide similar information, but they do vary in significant ways. The Lonely Planet series is called the "bible" by many backpackers since it includes lots of budget options. The DK Eyewitness Travel series is good for visual learners. The Rick Steves' series is excellent for Europe, the only continent they cover.

The best way to select a guidebook is to find one that fits your travel style. Start by getting your hands on a few different guides for a city in the United States that you know or a place abroad that you have been. You can often buy used guides or check them out from a library. Then see what format you like. If the book recommends things you like to do and places you would enjoy, then it may be a great guide for you to take abroad.

Free Online Resources
There are free online resources to aid in international travel planning. Two options are the Wikitravel website (www.wikitravel.org) and the Wikivoyage website (www.wikivoyage.org). Both are loaded with insider tips and are easy to use. Just go to the website and enter a country or city, and you instantly get pages of free information.

Travel Forums
Travel forums are websites where people post specific questions about a location. There are hundreds of forums to choose from. Dan and I have used the Lonely Planet Thorn Tree forum, the Travelfish

Asia travel forum, the Rick Steves' Travel Forum for Europe, Fodor's Travel Talk Forums, Trip Advisor Travel Forum, and Cruise Critic Message Board Forums (see the Resource List at the end of this chapter for website links).

If you sign up, you can post a question. Otherwise, you can search the discussions already there and may find an answer to your inquiry. The key is to find an active forum and preferably one that is professionally managed so someone is monitoring the answers. Also, check the dates of all posts and answers. A six-year-old response to a question similar to yours may not be accurate today.

Dan and I moderate a travel forum, the Wild Spirit Travelers Facebook group (www.facebook.com/groups/wildspiritravelers). Members post travel questions and answers, share useful travel articles or information on deals, and review travel products. Especially helpful are the conversations about what to see and do at a destination and the comments on what to avoid.

Chapter 1: Resource List

- ➢ Wild Spirit Travel's Travel Planning Checklist:
  www.wildspirittravel.com/book-checklist

- ➢ World Reviewer Holiday Weather Guide:
  www.worldreviewer.com/world-weather

- ➢ Temperature converter from Celsius to Fahrenheit:
  www.thecalculatorsite.com/conversions/temperature

- ➢ "Shoulder Seasons Around the World" by Jennifer V. Cole:
  www.travelandleisure.com/articles/shoulder-seasons

Chapter 1: Resource List (continued)

- ➤ Time and Date "Holidays and Observances around the World" page: www.timeanddate.com/holidays
- ➤ US Department of State: travel.state.gov
- ➤ Smart Traveler Enrollment Program: step.state.gov
- ➤ United Kingdom Foreign Travel Advice: www.gov.uk/foreign-travel-advice
- ➤ Wikitravel: www.wikitravel.org
- ➤ Wikivoyage: www.wikivoyage.org
- ➤ Lonely Planet Thorn Tree forum: www.lonelyplanet.com/thorntree/welcome
- ➤ Rick Steves' Travel Forum for Europe: www.ricksteves.com/travel-forum
- ➤ Travelfish Asia travel forum: www.travelfish.org/board
- ➤ Fodor's Travel Talk Forums: www.fodors.com/community
- ➤ Trip Advisor Travel Forum: www.tripadvisor.com/forumhome
- ➤ Cruise Critic Message Board Forums: boards.cruisecritic.com
- ➤ Wild Spirit Travelers Facebook group: www.facebook.com/groups/wildspirittravelers

Notes: _____

_____

_____

_____

Notes: _____

_____

_____

_____

_____

_____

_____

_____

_____

_____

_____

_____

_____

_____

Chapter Two

Travel Documents and Immigration

Traveling abroad requires more than just a plane ticket: you also need proper documentation. A passport is essential. Some countries also require a visa—not the credit card but the stamp you need to enter a foreign country.

We know a traveler who decided to go to Australia. She bought her plane ticket, made hotel reservations, and packed her bags. However, she did not research what travel documents she needed. When she showed up at the airport, she was shocked when the airline would not let her board because she did not have the required Australian visa. Wondering what you need for your international destination? This chapter addresses this and more.

Passport—Your Most Important Travel Document

One of the most important items to an international traveler is a passport. If you don't have one—get one. Don't wait until the last minute to apply. We have received a passport renewal in as little as two weeks, but we have also heard of it taking two months.

US passports are good for ten years (five for minors). [3] However, you may not be able to travel using your passport in the last few months of its validity. Even though it is still legal in the United States, some countries will not let you in if your passport is not valid for six months beyond your planned trip. Rules like this vary from country to country and are enforced by the country you are entering, not by the country that issues the passport. A good rule of thumb is to apply for a new passport at nine years. For more information on this topic, read "Your Passport May Not Be Valid for as Long as You Think" by Daniel Bare, on the Wild Spirit Travel website (www.wildspirittravel.com/your-passport-may-not-be-valid-for-as-long-as-you-think).

You may also need to get a passport early if you are an avid traveler and fill one up. Dan and I have done this. Some visas take just one corner of a page, while others can take two complete pages. If you are going to multiple countries, make sure you have enough empty pages.

---

3. "Frequently Asked Questions," US Department of State, accessed June 29, 2017, https://travel.state.gov/content/passports/en/passports/FAQs.html.

If you plan to travel abroad frequently, order the larger, nonstandard fifty-two-page passport. It is free when applying. At one time, people like me—who filled a regular twenty-eight-page passport—could get additional pages added for a fee. However, the US government no longer does this. If you fill up your passport, you need to get a new one.

Passport applications, along with full details on how to apply, are located on the US Department of State website (travel.state.gov/content/passports/en/passports.html). First-time applicants and travelers under eighteen must apply in person at a passport agency or passport acceptance facility.[4] Most passport renewals can be done via the mail.

Passport Cards
The US government also offers passport cards. They are cheaper than a passport book and are valid for the same amount of time. However, they only work at borders when traveling by car or boat to and from Mexico, Canada, the Caribbean, and Bermuda. They are not valid for air travel. As such, the passport card does not make sense for most international travelers.

Passport in the Clouds
Since a passport is one of the most important items for an international traveler, it is good to have a copy in case your original

4. "Apply for a Passport in Person," US Department of State, accessed June 20, 2017, https://travel.state.gov/content/passports/en/passports/applyinperson.html.

goes missing. If yours is lost or stolen, it is much easier to get a new one if you have a copy. Dan and I travel with our own copy, as well as one for each other. One of our travel secrets is also to make one color copy that you laminate. We have used this as identification when we have had to leave our real passport with a hotel or rental car agency abroad.

Dan and I also utilize the cloud by scanning our passports and saving the files to our cloud storage. Options include Dropbox, Google Drive, iCloud, as well as many other providers (see the Resource List at the end of this chapter for website links). If you have no cloud storage and do not have time to set one up, you can also scan your passport and email yourself the document. Then if you need it, you can open that email and print it off.

In addition to our passports, we save cloud copies of our travel visas, medical insurance cards, flight details, and other important documents we may need abroad. You may have some items stored on your phone, but what if that gets lost or your battery dies? It is best to have important information saved electronically, or a paper copy hidden away, so you can access it anywhere in the world.

Tourist Visas

There are many types of visas: work, student, retirement, etc. This book is for travelers, so in it we focus on tourist visas. This is the visa most travelers need to enter a country.

Do I Need to Get a Visa?

If you are wondering if you need a visa before traveling abroad, the answer is yes, no, maybe, and sometimes. There is no one answer; it all depends on the country you are visiting and your nationality. It is also important to know that requirements change. One year a country may not require a visa from American tourists, and the next year they do.

For American travelers, the best resource for determining if you need a visa is the US Department of State website (travel.state.gov). On the home page, do not go to the "US Visas" section—this is for travelers from other countries wanting to visit the United States. Instead, type your destination in the "Enter a Country or Area" box on the left side of the home page, and click Go. The following facts are provided for each country in the world:

- Passport validity
- Blank passport pages
- Tourist visa required
- Vaccinations (required to enter the country)
- Currency restrictions for entry
- Currency restrictions for exit

If a tourist visa is required, you can get more information by clicking the "Entry, Exit & Visa Requirements" plus sign. You can also obtain visa information at the government website for the country you plan to visit. However, the correct website for each country around the world may not be obvious. When Dan and I travel, we start with the US Department of State website and see if they provide a link to the website for the country we are traveling to. Often, they do.

How Do I Apply?

This is another question that has no simple answer. For many countries, tourists can show up at the airport or land border crossing and obtain the appropriate visa. However, some visas need to be acquired in advance. For these, some you can do online, some you mail in, and a few you must go to an embassy or consulate in person. Research this for every country you plan to visit before you go, and factor in the cost of visas to your travel budget. Some are free, but some cost hundreds of dollars.

Be leery of third-party agencies offering to get your visa for you; it can sometimes be a scam. However, some countries are now outsourcing the visa process, so going through a third party is legitimate. To know for certain, search the US Department of State website (travel.state.gov) for the country you plan to visit.

Important Visa Tips

Each country may impose a myriad of rules regarding their visa. For instance, some visas must be activated within thirty days of being stamped in your passport. Some require a letter of invitation or a hotel reservation. Some require proof of onward journey (e.g., transport out of the country). The list goes on. Do check on the countries you are traveling to.

Many countries require you to submit a passport-style photo to get a visa. If you are traveling long term to multiple countries, we recommend taking extra passport photos with you so you can get visas while abroad. However, sometimes this is not possible. Dan and I tried to visit both Russia and Brazil during our around-the-world trip. We were unable to get a visa for either, even though we visited their consulates in neighboring countries. When we were traveling, both nations required visas to be obtained from within your home country. For us, that meant in the United States, but since we were already off traveling, we could not send our passports back to America. So unfortunately, we were unable to visit either country.

Special European Visa

The Schengen Borders Agreement allows people to freely travel between participating European countries. US citizens may travel to these countries for up to three months without a visa. Crossing from one country to another does not restart the ninety-day countdown. There are twenty-six European countries that comprise the Schengen area: Austria, Belgium, Czech Republic, Denmark, Estonia, Finland, France, Germany, Greece, Hungary, Iceland, Italy, Latvia, Liechtenstein, Lithuania, Luxembourg, Malta, Netherlands, Norway, Poland, Portugal, Slovak Republic, Slovenia, Spain, Sweden, and Switzerland.[5]

---

5. "Schengen FAQs (Frequently Asked Questions)," US Department of State, accessed June 30, 2017, https://travel.state.gov/content/passports/en/go/schengen-fact-sheet.html.

As with all visa rules, things change. In 2017, travelers reported having to show their passports at some of the borders between Schengen-participating countries. This may or may not continue. The best rule for a traveler is to always be prepared and give yourself plenty of time to go through any border crossing.

Reciprocity Fees

Some countries charge reciprocity fees, even if they don't have a visa fee. This means if your country's government charges fees of people entering, they will charge you when entering their country. On one of our trips to South America, we discovered that many countries, including Argentina, had a 160 US dollar reciprocity fee on Americans. However, they granted an exemption from paying the fee, for US citizens in August 2016. Australian and Canadian passport holders still have a reciprocity fee.[6] This is another example of how entry requirements regularly change and need to be researched close to your time of travel.

Immigration and Customs

When you first arrive in a country, you will go through immigration and customs. This process is an important step. If you get it wrong, you may be denied entry into a country.

---

6. "Reciprocity Fee for US Citizens," Embassy of Argentina in the United States of America, accessed June 21, 2017, www.embassyofargentina.us/en/consular-section/reciprocity-fee-for-us-citizens.html.

Immigration

Immigration is about checking your travel documents and determining that you have a legitimate reason to enter a country. Even if you have a tourist visa stamped in your passport, the immigration officer at the border needs to be convinced that you are who you say you are (e.g., you look like your passport photo) and that you are entering their country for the purpose you say you are (e.g., to sightsee if on a tourist visa). A person entering as a tourist may be required to provide an address at which they are staying, show proof of funds, and have evidence of onward travel.

Going through Immigration

Here are some specific tips on how to go through immigration. First, as simple as this sounds, listen to the questions the immigration officer asks you. Then answer them truthfully, but do not elaborate or ramble on. Honestly answer each question, nothing more. Silence is okay; don't try to fill it up.

Not answering the question asked is a red flag. It's called avoidance, something border guards are trained to pick up on. Once I was asked at the Irish border how long I was going to be in the country. I was jet-lagged and hungry, and I was not really listening to the officer. Instead of answering the question, I said my goal was to go to Northern Ireland then cross over to Scotland. The next thing I knew, the officer had brought out a special stamp that he put in my passport. He then told me since I wanted to go to Scotland I best be off; he had only given me a visa to be in Ireland for twenty-four hours.

Oops! Yes, my goal was to go to Scotland, but I had wanted to spend a few days in Ireland first. Listen and answer what is being asked.

Arrival Card

For entry into most countries, you will need to fill out an arrival card. This is different from a visa. Travelers complete the arrival card at the border. If you are entering via a flight, the airline crew usually hands them out so you can complete it before landing. Each country's card is different, but most ask for standard identifiers (e.g., name, date of birth), duration of trip, port of embarkation (where you just came from), and what you are bringing into the country that customs should be aware of. Some ask for occupation and income. To see an example, read "Thai Immigration Card: What Is It and How to Fill It Properly" by Ivan Ramirez, on the Bangkok Has You website (www.bangkokhasyou.com/thai-immigration-card-tm6-what-is-it).

One tricky question, standard on arrival cards, has to do with the address in country. This may be tough to answer for two reasons: first, many tourists plan to travel around so do not have only one address. Still, for the card, just use where you are staying the first night. An immigration official can always ask you for more information if it's necessary to know where else you are going. This leads to the second difficulty: what if you have no reservation and are not sure where you are staying? We recommend that you enter a country with the name of one hotel where you could stay.

When Dan and I entered Albania, we had no idea where we were going. We came from Greece and had a vague plan to travel north. We did not know if we could get a bus on the same day we arrived, and if we could, how far north we could go. In anticipation of the where-are-you-staying question on the arrival card, before we left Greece, we researched the name of a hotel in the town where we were arriving. This is what we put on the form. It was an honest answer: if we were unable to journey onward that day, this was where we would have stayed. However, we were able to get a bus soon after arriving, so we did not stay there. The secret is to always have a travel plan when you go through immigration.

Keep that paper!

Sometimes when you go through immigration, the official will slip a card into your passport. Take a look at what it is. It may be very important, such as your departure card stamped with the date you must leave the country by. The official may not tell you what it is, but that doesn't mean it is not important. We have met numerous travelers who have tossed the card, only to learn they needed it when they went to leave the country. Without it, they had to pay extra fees.

Customs

Some people think immigration and customs are the same; however, they are not. Immigration is about checking whether you have a valid reason to be in the country, and customs is about what you are *bringing* into the country. At airports, you normally pass through immigration before baggage claim. Then you go through customs after baggage claim.

Going through Customs

Customs is concerned with making sure nothing is brought into the country that should not be. Some items, like certain drugs, are prohibited. Other items are restricted, and you need permission to bring them in. You should check the customs rules for the countries you are visiting before you go. For instance, Australia does not allow tourists to bring in steroids (even with a prescription), firearms (including paintball guns), meat products, or fruits and vegetables (including dried fruits like raisins).[7]

Many countries allow you to bring in limited amounts of alcohol, cigarettes, and general goods. Have too much, and they will want to tax you for it. If you bring in too many electronics, it also may raise questions. You should simply take what you need as a tourist. A laptop, tablet, and smartphone are considered reasonable, but three of each will raise a red flag.

In some countries, even dirt is restricted. On the arrival card for the United Kingdom, I once marked yes to having recently been on a farm. Therefore, the customs official had me take off my shoes and disappeared with them. After an extensive wait, in which I was starting to worry about what was going on, they returned with my now super-sanitized sneakers. They had washed my shoes to keep any farm dirt from entering their country.

---

7. "Can I Bring It Back?" Australian Government Department of Immigration and Border Protection, accessed July 09, 2017, www.border.gov.au/Trav/Ente/Brin/Can-I-bring-it-back.

To Declare or Not to Declare

When you leave baggage claim, there are often two options: the nothing-to-declare line and the to-declare line. Which should you walk through? Hopefully, you will have done research before you travel to know what you can take into a country. Assuming you have followed the rules, you will know which line is right for you. If, however, you are uncertain about something, then it is best to go through the declare line and ask an official.

For example, when Dan and I went to Australia, we knew they restricted some food items. We were entering with coffee beans, popcorn, and cookies. We did not know if these were fine or not, so we went in the declare line and were told we could keep the coffee and cookies, but they confiscated our popcorn. If we had gone through the nothing-to-declare line and they had found the popcorn, we would have faced fines and a lot of hassle.

Do know that customs officials have the right to search your bags when you enter a country. At many borders, people going through the nothing-to-declare line are randomly checked. Getting angry or annoyed at border officials is not advised and may lead to long delays, detention, or even denial of entry.

Traveling with Prescriptions

A customs consideration is traveling with prescription drugs. If you are traveling for one or two weeks, take all the drugs you need for your trip. Why waste a vacation day trying to figure out how to get more of your prescription? Most countries allow you to take the amount of your prescription needed for your stay, up to a ninety-day supply. Verify this for your destination.

If you are traveling longer than that, figure out where you will be when you need refills, and see what is required in that country. In many developing countries, you only need to go to the pharmacy and tell them what you want. In other countries, you have to see a doctor and get a local prescription.

Even if you don't think you will need a refill, travel with a prescription signed by your doctor. Some countries require this when you go through customs. I have been asked three times at customs to show my prescription. The signed prescription is also useful in case your drugs go missing or you drop them in a sink.

Never carry prescription drugs for someone else. The name on the prescription must be yours. The prescription should also indicate dosage, and it is best to have the generic name of the drug. For instance, Lipitor® is a brand name of a cholesterol-reducing drug; the generic name is atorvastatin.

Just because you have a prescription does not mean you can take that drug into every country. Some countries have banned-drug lists. Often, medications with codeine, pseudoephedrine, morphine, or dexamphetamine are banned. This means some pain medications, cold relievers, sleeping pills, and drugs used to treat attention deficit hyperactivity disorder (ADHD) may be illegal to take into some countries, even with a prescription. Most prescriptions are fine, as long as you have an actual written and signed doctor's note.

To check on a drug, contact the embassy for your destination. For more information on this topic, read "Traveling with Prescriptions: What NOT to Do" by Shyla Esko Bare, on the Wild Spirit Travel website (www.wildspirittravel.com/prescriptions).

If traveling with prescriptions drugs, as well as over-the-counter medicines or vitamins, it is important that a customs official can easily identify what you are transporting. As such, keep tablets separated and in labeled containers.

Chapter 2: Resource List

➢ "Your Passport May Not Be Valid for as Long as You Think" by Daniel Bare (July 11, 2016): www.wildspirittravel.com/your-passport-may-not-be-valid-for-as-long-as-you-think

➢ US passport information: travel.state.gov/content/passports/en/passports.html

➢ Dropbox: www.dropbox.com

➢ Google Drive: www.google.com/drive

➢ iCloud: www.apple.com/icloud

➢ Visa information for American citizens: travel.state.gov

➢ "Thai Immigration Card: What Is It and How to Fill It Properly" by Ivan Ramirez (October 13, 2016): www.bangkokhasyou.com/thai-immigration-card-tm6-what-is-it

➢ "Traveling with Prescriptions: What NOT to Do" by Shyla Esko Bare (July 13, 2017): www.wildspirittravel.com/prescriptions

Notes: _____

_____

_____

_____

_____

_____

_____

_____

_____

_____

_____

_____

_____

_____

_____

Chapter Three

Getting Money When Traveling

There is no denying that when you travel, you will need money to pay for things. How much you require depends on your destination, style of travel, and how many souvenirs you buy. Nevertheless, even frugal travelers need some money. This chapter discusses how to get that money when you are on the road.

ATMs Are the Way to Go

When Dan took his first international trip in the '80s and I took mine in the '90s, there were not many options for getting money overseas. For the most part, travelers had to take their funds with them. I went to Australia in 1990 with a stack of American Express® Travelers Cheques and my very first credit card (which I considered for emergencies only and never used).

Today, a traveler's ability to get money overseas is much easier. Automated teller machines (ATMs) are usually the best option. They keep your money in a safe place (the bank), so instead of carrying around thousands of US dollars, your money is safe.

However, do check before you travel to make sure that ATMs are the best option for you. First, verify there are ATMs where you are going. Most countries around the world have them, but in developing nations they may be scarce, and in rural villages nonexistent. Most importantly, confirm that there is an ATM in the location in which you are first arriving. According to their website, MasterCard® alone has over a million ATMs in 210 countries and territories worldwide. Nevertheless, you may still find yourself in an area without one. Dan and I did not encounter an ATM for days in countries like Mongolia, Bolivia, or Tanzania. To be sure that you will have access on your trip, check the MasterCard ATM Locator (www.mastercard.com/global/atmlocations) or the Visa® Global ATM Locator (www.visa.com/atmlocator).

Be aware that ATMs are not always 24/7. We needed an ATM in Luang Prabang, Laos, and could not find one our first day. It turns out that when the machine runs out of money, they simply put a board up in front of it so you can't even see it. Luckily, we had some local currency with us, and the machine was reopened before it was time to pay our hotel bill. Always have a backup plan, just in case an ATM is not working or out of money. We discuss how to have a plan B later in this chapter.

Mischievous Money Changers

At many borders, you will find *money changers*, people with stacks of money offering to swap the currency from the country you are leaving with the currency of the country you have just entered. In general, we are leery about using them. Dan and I have heard too many stories of people being shortchanged, given a bad rate, or receiving counterfeit bills. Plus, we don't feel safe changing money in the open where anyone can see how much money we have.

Sometimes money changers are the only option. Dan and I have crossed plenty of borders where there were no ATMs and we needed some local currency to pay for our onward journey. Our advice for using a money changer is to exchange as little money as you can. Do not try to hide it away in your security pouch when there are people around—this reveals where all your valuables are—but do put it in a secure place.

Not all border money changers are dodgy. In airports and train stations, you will often find automated money changers (that look like ATMs) or professional money-changer offices (that may look like a bank). There are often no safety risks at these; however, rarely do they give an exchange rate as good as a true bank ATM. We recommend using a bank ATM when possible.

Tips for Using ATMs Abroad

There are several special tips for using your ATM card abroad that all international travelers should know.

First, before you go, let your bank know you will be going overseas. If you don't tell them before you travel, your bank may see a foreign ATM charge, think it is fraud, and deactivate your card. You do not want that to happen when you are traveling.

Second, if your ATM personal identification number (PIN) is longer than four digits, change it to a four-digit number. Some foreign bank ATMs cannot handle a long PIN.

Third, if your bank has linked your checking and savings accounts, allowing funds to automatically transfer between the two, turn this feature off. In the very unlikely scenario that you are forced by a stranger to do an ATM withdrawal, you do not want all your money to be accessible. Dan and I put our travel funds in a special account that is not linked to any of our other accounts.

Lastly, it is very important that your ATM card is on the Cirrus® or Plus System, Inc (Plus) network. These are worldwide ATM networks. Some small banks and credit unions may not be associated with Cirrus or Plus, and their cards won't work overseas. We had a friend who visited us when we lived in Thailand. He brought an ATM card, but it was on the New York Currency Exchange (NYCE) network. That meant it did not work at all in Thailand, and he had no access to his money. Check your card before you go.

Breaking Big Bills

ATMs may give currency in notes that do not seem like a lot of money to a traveler, but they may be hard for small businesses to break. For instance, in Thailand, a 1,000-baht note may be difficult for a small merchant to make change for. It is only valued at about thirty US dollars; however, to a Thai vendor that charges twenty baht (about sixty cents) for a bowl of soup, it is huge. They often would not be able to make change for such a large note, so they usually will simply refuse the payment. And if you have already eaten the soup, then it is your responsibility to figure out a way to pay.

It is best to have small denominations of the local currency when you travel. The easiest way to get small bills is to use an ATM located at a bank. After you get your money, go into the bank and ask for smaller bills. Dan and I have done this at numerous banks in countries around the world and have always been given change with no hassle or fees.

Bank Fees Really Add Up

Bank fees are something to avoid when traveling, especially ATM charges. For an international withdrawal, usually the US bank *and* the foreign bank levy separate fees. Two payments for one withdrawal can really add up. In order to avoid fees, talk to all your banks and see which one has the lowest fees for where you are going. Some credit unions have no ATM fees, even abroad. Again, make sure they are on the Cirrus or Plus networks.

Also, try to reduce the number of ATM withdrawals you make by knowing the daily maximum you can take out in the local currency. Dan and I have stood at more than one ATM in a foreign country, having no idea how much we could withdraw because we did not know the exchange rate. Learn from our mistake—before you put your ATM card in the machine, know how much you can take out. A useful app to access current exchange rates while abroad is the XE Currency App (www.xe.com/apps). Once downloaded, you can use this free app off-line. More details on using this and other apps when traveling are included in the Wild Spirit Travel's Secrets to Using Technology Abroad class (www.wildspirittravel.com/courses).

As soon as you get the money, make sure you have a safe place to put it. If Dan and I are at an airport or a train or bus station, we will often grab the cash and go straight into separate restrooms. There, we each securely hide away the majority of the money in our money belts, only keeping out what is needed for that day. If I don't feel that I am in a safe situation, then I ignore the fees and withdraw only a small amount. Double bank fees may seem high, but compared to being robbed and losing all the money, it is not.

Charles Schwab Rebates ATM Fees

Before you travel abroad, you may want to open a Charles Schwab account. Charles Schwab is an online bank (www.schwab.com). They offer free Visa debit cards and rebate all ATM fees worldwide. Yup, you read right: they rebate *all* ATM fees worldwide. That means when you make a withdrawal from a foreign ATM, there will be a fee, but at the end of the month Charles Schwab will put it back in your account. This card is free; there is no minimum balance and no monthly service fee. It is our first-choice ATM card when we travel.

For information on other banks that don't charge foreign transaction fees, as well as a useful chart that compares fees for numerous banks and credit unions, read "Foreign ATM and Debit Card Fees by Bank" by Spencer Tierney and Jeanne Lee, on the NerdWallet website (www.nerdwallet.com/blog/banking/debit-card-foreign-transaction-international-atm-fees).

Credit Cards Abroad

Whether you will be able to use credit cards when you travel depends on the countries you visit and the style of travel you do. In most developed countries, you can use credit cards. However, you may not be able to use them for everything. In the States, you can make very small purchases on your credit card, but this is not the norm overseas. And not every place takes credit cards. Ask first. Many hotels in developed countries do, but not all. If you are staying in boutique places, guest houses, or bed and breakfasts, they may not. Dan and I have stayed in many guest houses in Europe where payment was cash only.

In developing countries, credit cards are not the norm, so expect to pay in local currency. High-end hotels and restaurants that cater to tourists may take credit cards, but it is not common. Do not plan to pay for meals, souvenirs, or transport using a credit card.

Even in developed countries, don't assume you can pay for transport, especially taxis, using credit cards. We know a traveler who had gone to Italy, where he took a taxi ride and then presented the driver with his credit card. The driver could not take it and got upset. The traveler had no euros, so he then tried to pay with US dollars. The driver refused with quite a bit of yelling and arm waving. In the end, the driver took the man to an ATM, but once paid he drove off, leaving the traveler there instead of his destination. Never assume you can use a credit card abroad.

Even though we do not plan to pay for things using credit cards, Dan and I always travel with them. They are great to have as an emergency backup. You can use them for cash advances or to pay for things online. For example, a hotel in a developing country may not be able to take credit cards in person, but you may be able to pay for your stay online using a card on a booking website.

MasterCard, Visa, or American Express?

Dan and I both take a MasterCard *and* a Visa credit card when we travel. In the United States, most places that take one, take both. However, overseas, this is not the case. If you see a MasterCard sign in the window, do not assume they also take Visa.

Many places worldwide do not take American Express or Discover® cards, so we don't recommend traveling with these as your only type of credit card. If they are the only credit cards you have, consider a prepaid MasterCard or Visa, which will be discussed later.

Declined

As we recommended for ATM withdrawals, always call your credit card providers to tell them you will be using your cards overseas. If you don't, then your charges may be denied. If you have reserved accommodations or overseas activities that will charge your card before your stay, let your credit card provider know that some charges may come in early. When asked for your travel dates, give yourself a cushion by saying you will be overseas a few days longer than planned. This is useful just in case your flight home is delayed.

Even after Dan and I notify our credit card companies, sometimes a charge will still be denied. This is especially true at the start of a trip. Carry your provider's phone number with you in case this happens. Many credit card companies have a toll-free number when calling internationally. If your card is denied, call that number as soon as you can and verify that you are overseas.

But what do you do in the moment? Imagine you are at a restaurant in Austria, Australia, or Argentina and the waiter informs you that your credit card has been denied. Do not get upset with the waitstaff—it is not their fault. Instead, carry some local currency for emergencies. Don't have any? We know one traveler in Belgium who simply asked to walk down the street to the ATM. The staff agreed, so he went and got money and came back and paid. He was lucky they were trusting.

PIN and Chip versus PIN and Signature
Even if you are at an establishment that takes MasterCard or Visa, your American credit card may not work. Many American credit cards are PIN and signature, whereas the norm in many countries is PIN and chip. Both technologies are more secure than the old magnetic swipe, but PIN and chip is the most secure because the card user must actually know the four- or six-digit PIN.

When using a credit card at restaurants in countries that use PIN and chip, your waiter will usually bring a card reader to your table. You then insert your card and enter your PIN. But what if you do not have a PIN? Well, that is when things get tricky. In some cases, you can press Cancel on the card reader then explain you will sign. Perhaps not the easiest thing if you are in a country where you do not speak the language. If the waiter does not understand or cannot accept PIN and signature, you are still liable to pay. Have cash just in case.

A few American banks have gone completely to PIN and chip, including the Charles Schwab card. We encourage you to think about getting a credit card that is PIN and chip. My top pick for a bank offering a PIN and chip card is Wells Fargo (www.wellsfargo.com). Other options include Andrews Federal Credit Union, Barclays, State Department Federal Credit Union, and United Nations Federal Credit Union. This is not an inclusive list. Before you change banks, call and ask if your credit card is PIN and chip or PIN and signature.

Just because you have a PIN associated with your credit card, it may not be a true PIN and chip card. Most credit cards work at ATMs, and those require PINs. With these cards, if a traveler enters the PIN at a restaurant, hotel, ticket kiosk, or anywhere they are making a regular credit card purchase, it is considered a cash advance. That means high interest fees from the moment the PIN is entered. Not a smart way to travel. So really understand what kind of credit card you have.

For more information on chip credit cards, read "Will Your Chip Credit Card Work Abroad?" by Shyla Esko Bare, on the Wild Spirit Travel website (www.wildspirittravel.com/will-your-chip-credit-card-work-abroad).

Traveler's Cheques: *Do* Leave Home without Them

Traveler's cheques used to be the best way to safely take money abroad, but not anymore. They are very difficult to cash. A few years ago, I tried cashing one in Buenos Aires. After being turned down by numerous banks, I finally went to a bank that actually sold them. Even they would not cash one. To avoid the hassle, we no longer recommend traveling with them.

Prepaid MasterCard and Visa Credit Cards

Prepaid MasterCard and Visas are a good option. Even for someone with regular credit cards, this can be a way to keep from overspending. Just put your vacation money on a prepaid card, and that is all you have for a trip. However, we advise taking another credit card and ATM card for emergencies.

Prepaid credit cards are readily available, but not every card is good for travelers. Some have high fees, are not reloadable (or not reloadable online), cannot be used outside the United States, or use magnetic-swipe technology. Read the fine print before purchasing.

For international travelers, we recommend finding a card that can be reloaded online and is PIN and chip. To be certain you purchase the right type of card, it may be easier to go into a bank rather than pick one up at a retailer. Wells Fargo has a prepaid card that is PIN and chip (www.wellsfargo.com/debit-card/chip-card-video). Another option is the MasterCard® Travelex Money Card (www.travelex.com/travel-money-card).

An important travel tip is that rental car companies often require a real credit card to rent a car. Prepaid cards and debit cards are generally not accepted.

Taking Foreign Currency with You

Dan and I are often asked if travelers should take foreign currency with them or get it abroad. The answer depends on how easily the currency is to get in the United States, what the fees and rates are to get it, and the traveler's comfort level on arriving with no local currency. We rarely get foreign currency before we go, because we are comfortable arriving without any cash and using an ATM when we first enter a country.

Our main reason for not getting currency before going overseas is the fees and rates. The fees vary between banks, credit unions, and AAA—some even offer no fees. However, if there are no fees, then often the rates are higher. In general, we do better using an ATM when we arrive at our destination, especially since we have no ATM fees on our Charles Schwab account. However, if we are not positive that an ATM will be readily available when we arrive, then we get some local currency before we go abroad. Wells Fargo (www.wellsfargo.com/foreign-exchange) has foreign currency available for over one hundred countries.

Have a Plan B

You should always have a backup plan for getting money when you travel. What happens if the only ATM in town is not working? What happens if your credit card company thinks there is fraud on your account and deactivates it? What happens if you lose your wallet with both your ATM card and credit card in it?

Dan and I travel with multiple sources for money. We use two banks in the United States so we can travel with two ATM cards. We keep one readily available and one locked up in our hotel safe or hidden away in our security pouches. We also travel with a MasterCard *and* a Visa credit card.

If your ATM card is your primary source for getting local currency, you need a plan if it does not work. One plan is to take a cash advance. Most credit cards allow cash advances from ATM or banks, and while this is a good option for emergencies, interest rates are often high. A pre-paid MasterCard or Visa is another good backup strategy.

Dan and I also travel with some US dollars. We do not expect to pay hotels, restaurants, or shops with our US money; however, when in a pinch, we have found having it useful. We exchange it at banks for local currency.

As a last resort, it is prudent to have a contact who could wire you money. There are Western Union offices in over two hundred countries and territories worldwide (locations.westernunion.com). We met a traveler in Bangkok who was crying outside of a hotel. She was unable to get money because her ATM card did not work and her credit card had been declined. She was jet-lagged, tired, and confused, and the hotel would not let her check in without leaving a key deposit, which she could not do without money. So, she sat on a Thai street corner crying. Not a good start to a vacation.

We helped her out by getting her checked in and discussing options. Since she was already abroad, she could not go back in time to open an account with a bank that was on the Cirrus or Plus network or notify her credit card company she would be abroad. She did call them, but they had already deactivated her card due to suspected fraud so they could only offer to send her a new card, which could take a week or longer. That left the option of getting money wired to her. Luckily, she had family that could access her bank account. They arranged for a Western Union transfer, and she had money the next day.

Keep Your Cash and Cards Safe

It is important to use smart travel strategies for keeping your cash and cards safe. Pickpockets often hang out around famous sights, since tourists make especially easy targets—they are distracted with sights, maps, and guidebooks. Crowded transport and busy markets are also prime pickpocket areas. To prevent a thief from ruining your vacation, follow these tips:

- Do not have all your money in one location. Have most stashed away and only some readily available.

- Do not keep your wallet in a back trouser pocket. Nor should you keep your money in a backpack or handbag worn at your back. These places are easy for pickpockets to get to.

- If in an area known for crime, keep a second wallet with an expired credit card and small amount of money in it. That way, if you are mugged, you have something to hand over.

Crossbody Day Bags

As for where to keep your actual credit card and money for the day, secure it in either a front zipper pocket in your clothes or in a crossbody day pack. Crossbody bags are better for traveling than a backpack, allowing you to keep the bag in front of you when walking and on your lap when seated. We know a tourist who had a backpack at a market in Thailand. He sat down for a meal and set the bag at his feet. When he finished eating, the food and the bag were gone.

The crossbody bag I use is the Travelon Anti-Theft Classic Crossbody Bag, which can be found on the Travelon website (www.travelonbags.com/anti-theft/classic/anti-theft-cross-body-bag). Other options we recommend are the Rick Steves' Veloce Guide Bag for iPad or the larger Veloce Shoulder Bag. Both are available at the Rick Steves' Travel Center in Edmonds, Washington, or at their online store (www.ricksteves.com/shop).

Security Pouches

Don't put all of your important stuff into your day bag. Instead, keep the truly valuable items to a traveler (e.g., passport, spare ATM and credit card, list of emergency contacts) in a hidden security pouch. This is worn under your clothes so no one can see it. If you need to get something out, don't do it in public. Instead, go into a restroom or somewhere else that is private and get what you need. I have seen tourists pull out their security pouches on the street to get a small amount of money to buy a soda. This is dangerous because they have shown all the pickpockets where their most important items are. Hidden security pouches are meant to stay hidden.

Lock Up Your Stuff

On travel days, you will need your passport. But if you are just spending a day in Paris, for instance, strolling around and admiring the Eiffel Tower, then leave your passport securely locked up in your hotel room. Some rooms have safes in them, and some offer safes through the front desk. You need to evaluate the option and decide if you think the safe is really secure. For one thing, make sure a room safe is actually bolted down so someone cannot just pick up the entire thing and walk out.

  If your room does not have a safe, or if it does but not one you feel is secure, then consider creating your own. Dan and I do this by first padlocking all the zippers on our bags. We then use a cable lock with a motion detector to lock our bags to something immovable in the room, such as a radiator or headboard. Sure, someone could slice into our bags, but the motion detector would go off if they did. We've used this trick for locking our bags up all around the world. We know of three times when an attempt was made to take our stuff (in Europe, Central America, and Asia), but our locks kept our bags safe. We sell a motion-detecting cable lock on our Wild Spirit Travel website (www.wildspirittravel.com/product/motion-detector-lock2).

We use this same system to lock our bags up on transport such as trains and buses. We met a few travelers who had their bags stolen on transport. One was on a train in Europe, when a man went to the toilet and left his backpack at his seat with a fellow traveler he had been talking to for hours. When he returned, it was gone. Another traveler told us how she slept soundly on a night bus in Argentina. Perhaps too soundly, for when she woke up, the bag she had put in the bin above her seat was gone. This is why we use a cable lock. On transport, however, we do not set the motion detector.

Leave Your Valuables at Home

One of our most important tips, when it comes to smart travel strategies, is not to travel with valuables. To a traveler, a passport seems like a valuable item, but it can be replaced. However, a piece of jewelry from your grandma may be irreplaceable. So, don't travel with it. On an international trip, I take nothing that I would fret about if it were lost or stolen. Dan even leaves his real wedding band at home and instead wears an inexpensive costume band with no sentimental value.

Chapter 3: Resource List

➤ MasterCard ATM Locator:
   www.mastercard.com/global/atmlocations

➤ Visa Global ATM Locator: www.visa.com/atmlocator

➤ XE Currency App: www.xe.com/apps

➤ Wild Spirit Travel's Secrets to Using Technology Abroad
   class: www.wildspirittravel.com/courses

➤ Charles Schwab online bank: www.schwab.com

➤ "Foreign ATM and Debit Card Fees by Bank" by Spencer
   Tierney and Jeanne Lee (January 12, 2017):
   www.nerdwallet.com/blog/banking/debit-card-foreign-
   transaction-international-atm-fees

➤ Wells Fargo: www.wellsfargo.com

➤ "Will Your Chip Credit Card Work Abroad?" by Shyla Esko
   Bare (April 26, 2016): www.wildspirittravel.com/will-your-
   chip-credit-card-work-abroad

➤ Wells Fargo prepaid PIN and chip credit card:
   www.wellsfargo.com/chip-card/chip-technology-video/

➤ MasterCard®Travelex Money Card: www.travelex.com/travel-
   money-card

➤ Wells Fargo Foreign Exchange:
   www.wellsfargo.com/foreign-exchange

➤ Western Union offices: locations.westernunion.com

➤ Travelon Anti-Theft Classic Crossbody Bag:
   www.travelonbags.com/anti-theft/classic/anti-theft-cross-
   body-bag

Chapter 3: Resource List (continued)

- ➤ Rick Steves' Velocé Guide Bag for iPad or Velocé Shoulder Bag: www.ricksteves.com/shop

- ➤ Motion-detecting cable lock: www.wildspirittravel.com/product/motion-detector-lock2

Notes: _____

_____

_____

_____

_____

_____

_____

_____

_____

_____

_____

_____

Notes: _____

_____

_____

_____

_____

_____

_____

_____

_____

_____

_____

_____

_____

Chapter Four

It's a Small World—with Many Languages

Dan and I love the idea of learning the local language when we go abroad. However, in our travels to more than seventy countries, we have experienced thirty-nine major languages and hundreds of minor ones. Nope, we don't speak thirty-nine languages. I speak two— English and Spanish. Dan speaks English, plus some French, Spanish, and Thai.

When we visit a country, we try to learn a few words of the local language. We find it fun, polite, and a way to make friends with the locals. Luckily, doing this has become increasingly easy in this technological age.

Phrase Books

Phrase books, used to be the best option for travelers. Some people still travel with them, but we don't. The problem with phrase books is you don't actually hear how a word is pronounced. Dan and I have confused more than one local by mispronouncing words read out of a phrase book. Even if you can pronounce the words, phrase books are often limited to tourist talk.

You can find free language phrase books online at Wikitravel (wikitravel.org/en/list_of_phrasebooks) and at Wikivoyage (en.wikivoyage.org/wiki/phrasebooks). They usually have grammar rules that help with basic pronunciation and reading. We sometimes print out these rules and travel with them.

Translation Apps

There is an incredible free translation app called Google Translate. Use it on your laptop, tablet, or smartphone. The Google Translate app is constantly increasing its functionality and the number of languages it translates—103 at last count.

On your desktop, go to the Google Translate website (translate.google.com), and type or say what you want translated. You can see it written out, or listen to it by pressing the microphone. Easy enough; however, most of us do not travel with our laptop.

Fortunately, you can also download the Google Translate app for free to your smartphone. You can type a sentence in English and see it translated in the language you choose, or you can say it in English and then listen to the translation by pressing the button that looks like a speaker. For some languages, you can do both of these off-line as long as you have downloaded the language pack.

The most amazing feature of the Google Translate app is the instant-camera option. You open the app, choose a language with this feature and, if you have downloaded the language pack, press the button in the app that looks like a camera. Then hold your phone up to a sign, and it instantly translates the sign into English. It is like magic! Imagine seeing a sign in an Amsterdam train station and you have no idea what it says. Then you follow these steps, and suddenly your phone shows you that the sign says "Exit to street." I have been astounded by this app around the world.

It works best on signs or menus. It does not translate newspapers or books very well. But for a tourist, it does the trick and is one of the best tools a traveler can take abroad. There are currently twenty-nine languages with the instant-camera option that can be downloaded and used off-line.

Learning Languages

Although useful, translation apps are a bit of a cheat. It means you can get by as a tourist, but it does not mean you can speak to the locals. If you want to go deeper with a language, consider a language-learning program.

Adult-language-learner expert Emily Liedel recommends the Pimsleur® language programs (www.pimsleur.com). They are available in a myriad of languages. If you're not sure how committed you are to learning a language, see if your library has Pimsleur courses available to check out. For useful tips on learning a new language as an adult, visit Emily Liedel's Babel Times website (www.thebabeltimes.com). She also has a book called *Beyond Bilingual*, available through her website.

Duolingo

Duolingo is a language-learning website and app, free on iPhones and Androids (www.duolingo.com). It offers education in twenty-three languages. This app is especially useful if you have some knowledge of a foreign language and are trying to brush up or increase vocabulary.

English Abroad

For those of us with English as our first language, we are very lucky when traveling abroad. In many parts of the world, English is the language of the tourist industry. Although a traveler can often get by completely in English, this is not always the case.

If you are in a country where English is not an official language, don't expect everyone to speak English simply for your convenience. Understand that when traveling in a foreign country, it is your responsibility to get your needs across—not the job of locals to understand English. It is also important to keep your voice at a speaking level. If you encounter someone who does not understand when you speak English in a normal tone, then believe me, that person is not going to understand you when you shout.

Instead, be prepared to pantomime what you need. Hopping on one foot and squatting a bit has always gotten me directed to a toilet. And remember, a smile and friendly demeanor go a long way in getting people to want to help you. Sometimes all it takes is context. Dan and I went into a Vietnamese restaurant well off the tourist track. No one spoke English, but the staff could pretty easily figure out we wanted food. One waiter led us into the kitchen where he lifted the lids off various pots, then we pointed to what looked good and were served a delicious meal.

Ten Key Words

When possible, Dan and I try to learn a few key words in the local language. The ten we focus on are:

- Hello
- Please
- Thank you
- Excuse me
- Yes
- No
- Goodbye
- Water
- Toilet
- Cheers

We like to use the Google Translate app to learn these words before we go abroad. We have also found that practicing them on a long-haul flight is a great use of our time.

You can do a lot with these ten words. Dan also likes to learn to say *how much*. He finds this useful when negotiating prices in markets. I get anxious when I say it, because I often can't understand the reply. Instead, I like to travel with a small calculator. I'll type in a number and hand it to the vendor. The vendor will type in a counteroffer, and we negotiate through the calculator. Yes, my smartphone has a calculator option, but I don't want to hand this to strangers around the world.

Count to Ten

Talking about numbers, it is helpful to be able to count to ten in the local language. Luckily, most of the world uses Arabic numerals (e.g., 1, 2, 3), the same that Americans use, so you should be able to read a price if posted.

However, some Arabic countries use Eastern Arabic numerals, and they look very different (see a comparison at en.wikipedia.org/wiki/eastern_arabic_numerals). If you are going to a Middle Eastern country, it is helpful to be familiar with these numbers. Dan is better about learning them than I am, and it came in handy when we traveled to Egypt. Many places had prices posted in only Eastern Arabic numerals, and if I asked the price, I was often told a higher amount than was posted. But then Dan would point at the sign and say their posted price, as he could read it, and they would sheepishly charge us that.

Tricks to Learning Languages

Dan and I also try to find mnemonic devices (word-association tricks) for these key words. For example, when I tried to learn the Greek word *efharisto*, which means *thank you*, I really struggled. I never seemed to remember it when testing myself on the ten key words. When I mentioned my struggle to a Greek hotel employee, he said that actually it was an easy word to pronounce as it sounded a lot like *a ferry stone*. It did, and this I could remember. After that, when I wanted to say thanks in Greece, I would say, "a ferry stone" really fast with the words squished together. The locals understood, and many told me they appreciated the effort.

Create a Cheat Sheet

Foods are also useful words to learn when traveling. You eat three meals a day, so food is important. The Google Translate app is great with menus. But if you don't want to always use your phone, or if you are in a country that speaks a language not translated by Google, then think about making a cheat sheet. It is useful to have a small list of foods you love and hate in the local language.

If you have any food allergies, it is extremely important that you are able to tell people what you are allergic to. Make yourself a card for this. I traveled in Europe with my sister, who is allergic to citric acid. She made cards in the language of each country we visited that listed every food she could not have. Whenever she ordered food, she would hand the waiter the card. You don't want to pantomime allergies, so do this before you go to make sure you have the translation correct.

Get a Note from Your Hotel

If you find yourself somewhere without a working translation app and you need something specific in a foreign language, ask your hotel staff to write you a note. In China, Dan had the hotel staff write him a note describing how he wanted his hair cut. It said 回到后面，which means *short in back*, or at least Dan hoped it did because he could not read the message. When he entered the Beijing barbershop, the staff looked worried, until he handed them the note. Then there were smiles all around, and Dan got a great haircut. We have never had hotel staff refuse to write out instructions for us, so utilize them.

Dual Language Business Cards

Talking about hotels, it is important to know the name of your hotel in the local language. Not a westernized or tourist name, but the local name a taxi driver will understand. In some countries, hotels have two names: one they give foreigners and one in the local language. If you have a business card with only the name for foreigners, a taxi driver may not be able to drive you there. Make sure a card is dual language or just in the local language.

Chapter 4: Resource List

➢ Wikitravel language phrase books: wikitravel.org/en/list_of_phrasebooks

➢ Wikivoyage language phrase books: en.wikivoyage.org/wiki/phrasebooks

➢ Google Translate app: translate.google.com

➢ Pimsleur® language programs: www.pimsleur.com

➢ *Beyond Bilingual* by Emily Liedel, plus other tips for adult language learners: www.thebabeltimes.com

Chapter 4: Resource List (continued)

➢ Duolingo language-learning app: www.duolingo.com

➢ Eastern Arabic numerals:
en.wikipedia.org/wiki/eastern_arabic_numerals

Notes: _____

_____

_____

_____

_____

_____

_____

_____

_____

_____

_____

_____

_____

Notes: _____

_____

_____

_____

_____

_____

_____

_____

_____

_____

_____

_____

Chapter Five

Travel Health before Your Trip

The information in this book is not intended or implied to be a substitute for professional medical advice, diagnosis, or treatment. Dan and I are not doctors. We are simply travelers who have encountered health issues while abroad. Never disregard professional medical advice or choose not to consult with a medical provider before or during a trip because of something you have read in this book. Dan and I have seen doctors around the world, and we encourage you to do so as well.

Lessening Jet Lag

Jet lag is a before-you-go issue, since international travelers should have a strategy for their flight before they fly. Jet lag depends on the direction and distance you travel. The more time zones you cross, the tougher it is on the body and mind.

West Is Best

There is a saying: *west is best, east is a beast*. On our first around-the-world trip, Dan and I flew east and learned the hard way how true this saying is. Since then, we have flown west around the globe. Of course, most travelers are not flying around the world, which means at some point they will be flying east. For example, most Americans fly east when going to Europe and west when coming home.

There is no foolproof way to avoid jet lag, but you can take steps so it is not as bad. First, adjust your schedule at home the week before you go. If you are flying east, then go to bed earlier and earlier. If you are going west, stay up late for a few nights.

Second, have a game plan for the flight, based on when you will land at your destination. If you are landing in the morning, try to get your night's sleep on the plane. Pop on eyeshades and earplugs, and go to sleep. Don't concern yourself with the in-flight meal or movie. If you can't sleep, stay in a restful pose.

On the other hand, if you are landing in the evening, stay awake for the flight so you can go to sleep soon after you arrive. If you sleep too much on the flight, you may not be able to sleep at your destination. Nap if you need to, but watch the movie, chat with your neighbor, indulge in the honey-roasted peanuts. If you stay awake on the flight, keep yourself hydrated. Airplanes can dry you out, so drink water.

Third, when the airplane takes off, change your watch. As soon as wheels are up, consider yourself in the time zone of your destination. On a recent flight, I was not able to do this because my watch pairs with my cellular phone, and it did not switch times until I landed and got a Wi-Fi connection. If you have a watch like this, research how to manually change the time before you go.

At Your Destination

Once you arrive, get on the local schedule as soon as you can, but don't be crazy about it. If you arrive in the morning and need a nap that afternoon, take one. Just set your alarm so you wake up in an hour or two. Do not take a nap until midnight; if you do, you will not be switching to the local time zone.

How Many Shots Does a Traveler Need?

Getting vaccinated is a personal choice, and one you should discuss with your medical provider. Not everyone should get every vaccine, and some have side effects that you should know about before getting the shot or taking the tablet.

There is health information for each country on the US Department of State website (travel.state.gov). More comprehensive information can be found through the Centers for Disease Control and Prevention (www.cdc.gov). The website has a "Travelers' Health" section, where you can search any country to find out if there are any current health concerns or issues.

Another good resource is Scotland's National Health Service website called Fit for Travel (www.fitfortravel.nhs.uk). I especially like the maps in the "Malaria" section, which let you see what areas of a country malaria is an issue (often it is not everywhere). On a trip to Vietnam, we decided to avoid malaria-affected zones so we would not have to take malaria tablets. We used the Fit for Travel maps to determine where we could travel to and where we should avoid.

Maddening Mosquitoes

Mosquitoes can be annoying anywhere, but we find them especially irksome when on holiday. Especially since mosquitoes can spread diseases like dengue fever—something I experienced in Thailand. Unfortunately, there is no vaccine for dengue, nor is there one for malaria. However, there are preventative measures a traveler can take to avert dangerous mosquito-borne illnesses.

The main prophylaxis is not to get bitten by a mosquito. For tips on avoiding bites, read "4 Tips for Mosquito Free World Travel" by Shyla Esko Bare, on the Wild Spirit Travel website (www.wildspirittravel.com/4-tips-for-mosquito-free-world-travel). If visiting an area of the world with malaria mosquitoes, you should consult your doctor or go to a travel clinic before you go abroad. The recommended tablets for malaria will vary based on destination and your health, so have a professional advise you on this.

Yellow Fever

Yellow fever is also a mosquito-borne illness. However, there is a vaccine for it, and it is the only inoculation that may be required of international travelers. Countries that have the potential for yellow-fever cases may require a visitor to get the shot; however, even if that country does not require the vaccination, the next destination might. When Dan and I went to Kenya—a country with yellow fever—we were not required to have the vaccination to visit. Nevertheless, we had to get it because our next destination, India, required anyone coming from Kenya to be inoculated.

For information on active or potential yellow-fever areas, read "Yellow Fever: A Current Threat" on the World Health Organization website (www.who.int/csr/disease/yellowfev/impact1/en). If you are visiting a yellow-fever region, check that country's vaccine requirement and your next destination's requirement at the Centers for Disease Control and Prevention website (www.cdc.gov).

Travel Insurance—To Get or Not to Get

Dan and I are regularly asked if we recommend travel insurance. Yes, we do, but it is not a simple yes or no. Travel insurance encompasses many things, the two main areas being medical insurance abroad and dealing with canceled tours, lost baggage, delayed flights, and stolen property. We do not always purchase insurance for transport delays; however, we like to have the electronics we travel with insured and would not travel overseas without medical coverage.

Our decision to insure our transport depends on whether we think being delayed will be an actual inconvenience. When traveling long term, a delayed flight is often not a big deal for us. However, if we are on a two-week holiday and have to get back to work, then we will consider insurance. If we want coverage, we check to see if our credit card offers any. If it does, we'll use it to book our transport or tour. Check your credit cards to see if there is any built-in insurance.

Property you travel with, such as electronics, may be covered under your homeowner insurance policy. Ask your agent before you go. You should also check with your current medical insurance to see if there is any overseas coverage and to what degree. Dan and I traveled once with a medical plan that had overseas coverage, but it only covered emergencies abroad, and then only if we notified the company within twenty-four hours of seeking care.

In some countries, hospitals require a traveler to submit a passport in order to get care. They return it only when your bill is paid. And just because you have insurance does not mean the foreign hospital will take your card and bill the insurance for you. You may have to pay up front for medical care, then after your trip submit the bills and claim reimbursement.

If you do not have medical insurance that covers you overseas, then consider travel insurance. Even if you have some coverage through your current plan, it may not include evacuation back to the United States for care. We recommend having this.

Travel insurance is often reasonably priced. Dan and I recently took out a plan for a month of travel that covered stolen property, lost bags, and emergency medical—including evacuation for the injured and a travel companion—at the low cost of forty US dollars. We found and purchased this plan through SquareMouth (www.squaremouth.com), a website that compares multiple insurance options so you can find the one best suited for your trip. For a quote, go directly to their website or find a link on the Wild Spirit Travel "Resources" page (www.wildspirittravel.com/resources).

Nix Motion Sickness

If you are prone to motion sickness, as I am, have a plan before you go. I did a tour with my mom of the Czech Republic, Austria, and Hungary. Numerous times, I had to ask the driver to stop the bus so I could stand at the side of the road and get my equilibrium back. It was either that, or throw up in my seat. Finally, one of the other passengers offered me their spare acupressure bracelet. It made all the difference, and the tour could finally travel without making special stops for me.

Since then, I have discovered the combination of products that work for me in nixing motion sickness. I wear an acupressure bracelet, and if I start to feel nauseous, I suck on a ginger candy. I have been told that the fact these remedies work is all in my head, but then motion sickness is just in my head, so that is fine with me. The brand of acupressure bracelet I wear is BioBands, which can be found on their website (www.biobands.com).

Squash Travel Phobias

If you have a phobia that might impact your travels, deal with it before you go. I had a pretty strong fear of heights, so much that when I went to the Eiffel Tower, I got off the elevator at the top, started screaming, and had to be taken straight back down on the next elevator. Not fun. But since then, I have seen a hypnotherapist, and I can now go into tall buildings. In fact, I zip-lined in Costa Rica, had dinner in the Sky Tower in New Zealand, and went hang gliding in Chile. All activities I could not have done before dealing with my fear of heights. So, address your travel-related phobias before you go.

Street-Food Savvy

Another way to stay healthy on a trip is to eat well. Dan and I definitely eat street food when we travel; however, we are smart about it. We look for stalls frequented by locals and ones that cook the food right there. We don't eat food that has been sitting out for hours on end. Also, in countries where it is unsafe to drink the water, we avoid foods that may have been made with local water.

Find a Happy Cow

If you are vegetarian or vegan, a great way to find food abroad is the Happy Cow website (www.happycow.net). It is a free app that lists vegetarian and vegan-friendly restaurants, shops, and more around the world. Even meat eaters who are looking for a healthy meal can benefit from this app.

Chapter 5: Resource List

> ➢ US Department of State health information: travel.state.gov
> ➢ Centers for Disease Control and Prevention: www.cdc.gov
> ➢ Scotland's National Health Service Fit for Travel website: www.fitfortravel.nhs.uk

Chapter 5: Resource List (continued)

➢ "4 Tips for Mosquito Free World Travel" by Shyla Esko Bare (August 17, 2015): www.wildspirittravel.com/4-tips-for-mosquito-free-world-travel

➢ "Yellow Fever: A Current Threat" by World Health Organization: www.who.int/csr/disease/yellowfev/impact1/en

➢ SquareMouth travel insurance: www.squaremouth.com

➢ Wild Spirit Travel "Resources" page: www.wildspirittravel.com/resources

➢ BioBands acupressure bracelets: www.biobands.com

➢ Happy Cow: www.happycow.net

Notes: _____

_____

_____

_____

_____

_____

_____

_____

_____

Notes: _____

_____

_____

_____

_____

_____

_____

_____

_____

_____

_____

_____

Chapter Six

Tours or DIY Travel

One decision to make before going abroad is whether to travel with a tour or on your own. Tours are easy because the company coordinates activities, lodgings, and transport. However, some are sterile or expensive. Although Dan and I usually prefer to travel independently, we have done some amazing group tours. If you want to go with a group, then choose your tour wisely. Don't base it only on price; look for a tour that will give you the experience you want—whether it be adventurous, posh, cultural, relaxing, educational, experiential, gastronomical, historic, or some combination.

If, like Dan and I, you like the idea of independent travel where you manage all aspects of the trip, then do-it-yourself (DIY) travel may be a better fit. This chapter covers the pros and cons of tours versus DIY travel.

Talented Travel Agents

Dan and I are often asked if travel agents still exist, since travelers can book most any tour, transport, or accommodation themselves via the Internet. Be assured, travel agents do exist, and they provide a valuable service. Travel agents research rates and develop industry relationships, which can get their clients great deals. Travel agents can save a traveler time, money, and hassle.

The key to working with a travel agent is to find someone who really understands the type of trip you want. Use an agent who listens to you and presents a customized plan instead of shoehorning you into one with the highest commission. Three travel planners who impress us are Anne Berry and Angela Jacobus, co-owners of Travel That Matters (www.travelthatmatters.net), and Mary Cecchini, travel designer of Living Big (www.livingbig.org/traveldesign).

Being in the travel industry, Dan and I have met many other travel agents over the years and have a list of ones we recommend. For contact details, visit the Wild Spirit Travel "Resources" page (www.wildspirittravel.com/resources). Don't just use one because of our recommendation; talk to a few and find the best match for you. Personally, we like agents who are travelers themselves, ones who can relate to our desire to take cultural trips that let us meet locals, try regional foods, sightsee at a slow pace, have serendipitous adventures, and get some pampering, too.

Terrific Tours

Travel agents can book a tour for you—or you can find options in guidebooks or online searches. There are many to choose from, and there is not one tour company that is ideal for every traveler. If you decide to book your own tour, do your research and read reviews. Also, ask other travelers how their experiences were with a particular tour company, by using travel forums like TripAdvisor (www.tripadvisor.com/forumhome) or the Wild Spirit Travelers Facebook group (www.facebook.com/groups/wildspirittravelers).

Just because a company gets rave reviews, it is not a guarantee that you will have a good time. A major factor in satisfaction is finding a tour that meets your style, personality, and demographic. There are tours for under thirty-year-olds and for over sixty-year-olds. There are tours that visit multiple sights a day and tours that visit fewer sights as a group and encourage participants to go off and have their own adventures. Be clear on the type of tour you want before you book.

Also, be very clear as to what you get for your money. Some tours are all inclusive, while others do not provide meals or entrance fees to sights. What may seem like a good value when you book may turn out to be a financial stretch if you have to pay for everything at the destination.

Size Is Important

With tour companies, size is important. Dan and I consider a group of fifteen or less to be a small-group tour, but we have heard of tours with as many as twenty-five still labeling themselves as *small group*. We feel like that is a midsize tour and over forty is large. Some tours aim for fifty-plus travelers.

Is small better on a tour? That depends on the traveler. The first tour I did was with my sister. We were in our twenties and did a ten-day, seven-country tour of Europe with Contiki (www.contiki.com). There were thirty travelers, all under thirty-five, as Contiki tours are for eighteen- to thirty-five-year-olds. We had a great time meeting the other travelers and seeing so many places.

Would I take that tour today? No way, and not just because I am over Contiki's age range. My travel style has changed. I now prefer small groups that focus more on traveling slow and truly experiencing the culture while meeting locals. This does not mean I will never do a midsize or large tour again. At some point that may be what I am looking for. Each time you book a tour, consider what you want on that trip.

Hand-Holding versus On Your Own

Tours vary greatly in the amount of guidance they give you. On some, the tour leader stays with you every day, all day. On others, the tour guide simply points you in the right direction then lets you explore on your own. Neither option is *correct* for all travelers—just be aware that this varies, and find a tour that provides the level of support you want for that trip.

Tour Companies Here, There, and Everywhere

Tour companies also differ based on where they are located and how many places they cover. You can book with a company based in your country, the country you are visiting, or a global corporation with numerous offices around the world. One example of a US-based tour company that we recommend is Rick Steves' Europe (www.ricksteves.com). The company is based in Washington State and only does tours to Europe. My brother has done several Rick Steves' tours and has loved them.

An example of an *everywhere* corporation is G Adventures (www.gadventures.com). We have not used them but would consider it because of the many rave reviews from travelers we know. G Adventures is based in Canada. It has twenty-three offices around the world and leads tours in over one hundred countries.

Still, Dan and I prefer to do tours that are *there*. By that we mean tours that are based in the country we are going to and only service a small region. We like having indigenous guides and knowing that our tourist dollar is helping the local infrastructure. When traveling long term, we often have flown to a destination and then arranged our tour there. If time is limited, we do this before our trip. We have found the Wikitravel website (www.wikitravel.org) and the Wikivoyage website (www.wikivoyage.org) especially useful in finding local tour companies.

One example of a local company we have used is Sam's Bungalow in Bukit Lawang, Indonesia. We booked a jungle trek directly with Sam (www.samsbukitlawang.com), upon which we saw orangutans, leaf monkeys, macaques, and gibbons. The tour was amazing, and we enjoyed knowing that our tourist dollar went straight to Sam and his family.

Responsible Travel and Voluntourism

Some operators offer tours that positively impact the local people and communities. Dan and I find tours of this nature through Responsible Travel (www.responsibletravel.com). They list only tours that give back to the local community in some way. It is a UK website, so prices are often listed in pound sterling. Use the XE currency conversion website to find its equivalent in US dollars (www.xe.com).

It was through Responsible Travel that Dan and I discovered Njari Lodge and Campsite. Located in a remote village high on the slopes of Mount Kilimanjaro, this locally owned ecolodge had no electricity or running water. What it did have was friendly staff, daily activities that benefited numerous village businesses, and amazing views of Mount Kilimanjaro. The cost of just eleven dollars a night included three meals a day. Each day, our guide bought ingredients from a different farmer, so the "wealth" was distributed around the village. And they employed a widow to do the laundry—giving her a way to have an income and support her family.

Voluntourism, which refers to trips that incorporate volunteer work abroad, is popular. Dan and I advise researching this type of trip before you book. Some are authentic and doing good work, but others are simply about lining the pocket of the middleman and do little to actually help. *The Volunteer Traveler's Handbook* by Shannon O'Donnell is a great resource for finding ethical volunteer opportunities around the world.

Recommended by Wild Spirit Travel

Volunteer Voyages (www.volunteer-voyages.com) is a tour company Dan and I recommend for volunteer travel. It is an authentic tour company that does small volunteer-based trips. The owner spends time with locals to determine the best ways tour groups can actually help in long-term and sustainable ways.

There are other tours and guides that offer trips that help the areas they journey to. Many specialize (e.g., women-only tours, trips designed for travelers over fifty). To see a list of responsible tours that we endorse, visit the Wild Spirit Travel "Resources" page (www.wildspirittravel.com/resources).

DIY Travel

Most often, Dan and I travel independently. We enjoy planning our own trips and discovering the wonders of a destination that interest us the most, not the ones every tour company visits. We tend to travel slow, really delving into cultures. DIY travel does have its challenges—we have been lost more than once. Nevertheless, we find it rewarding and a fun way to travel.

Do What Is Unique around the World

Wondering what to do in Mexico, Monaco, Morocco, or Mongolia? I can tell you what Dan and I enjoyed doing in each of these countries, but that may not be what you want to do at all. In order to have the trip of *your* dreams, you have to do the things *you* find amazing, not just what someone else tells you to do.

We advise travelers to do what is unique for the location they visit, whether it is a museum, historic sites, specialized lodgings, or its natural beauty. For example, the Museum of New Zealand Te Papa Tongarewa (www.tepapa.govt.nz), in Wellington, New Zealand, has exhibits covering a range of subjects including Renaissance art. However, we skipped that section, because we go to galleries filled with Renaissance art when we are in Europe. Since we were in New Zealand, we focused on the floor that exhibited Māori art and culture. There is no museum in the world that covers Māori art as well as in New Zealand, so that is the place to see it.

If you try to see and do everything everywhere, you will wear yourself out. You can only see so many waterfalls, so visit ones that are truly wondrous not just trickles. And sleep in a traditional *ger* (also known as a yurt) in Mongolia, not Mexico.

Local Interactions

An important part of traveling—if you want to learn about cultures and not just see sights—is to interact with the locals. Step off the tourist route and discover how natives live. Some tours include meeting with locals or staying in their homes. This is great, even if a bit contrived since these people may be paid to interact with you.

You may be able to experience real culture by using free time on a tour to go down side streets and find places where locals are hanging out. If you are not on a tour, then this is even easier. Go explore. Don't stop at the restaurant right at the Eiffel Tower just because they have a menu in English. Instead, walk a few streets away and go someplace where there is no menu at all.

Eating and Cooking with Locals

Eat with a Local (www.eatwithalocal.com), offers a way to meet people when you travel and share a meal. Some hosts invite you to their home to cook for you, while others offer to meet you at a restaurant and explain the local cuisine. Although we have not personally used this, we have heard great reports from travelers who have. Of note, neither hosts nor travelers are vetted, so use common safety sense, especially for solo travelers.

Another great way to eat with locals is to take a cooking class as you travel. There are group and private classes in many countries around the world. Tour or travel agents can often help you find these, or visit the Traveling Spoon website (www.travelingspoon.com).

Free Walking Tours

One of our favorite things to do in a foreign city is a walking tour. In Europe, a great option is Sandemans New Europe free walking tours (www.neweuropetours.eu). The company operates in eighteen cities and provides what they call *infotainment* by mixing history with charismatic storytelling. Dan and I have found the guides to be fun and willing to talk about their culture, and we have always happily tipped the guide at that end of the tour.

Find a Local Guide

You can learn about life in the country you are visiting by hiring a native guide. We were quite happy with guides from the Viator website (www.tourguides.viator.com). However, our experience was before the company was bought by Trip Advisor in 2014, and we have since noticed the prices seem to be considerably higher. That said, their guides continue to get five-star reviews, so if one is in your budget it may be a great option. Similarly, try Tours by Locals (www.toursbylocals.com).

Volunteer Guides for a Better World

In chapter 7, we discuss Servas International (www.servas.org), which is a nonprofit that promotes world peace through travel, as a home-stay resource. Most Servas hosts offer free lodgings, but some are day hosts and volunteer guides instead. Day hosts will meet you, for free, to talk about their life, city, culture, and so forth. Dan and I are members of Servas United States (www.usservas.org). We have learned more about local life around the planet by meeting Servas hosts than by looking at famous sites. We highly recommend that you join, so you can learn about other cultures when traveling abroad, as well as host members who come to your city. Dan and I find it fun and enlightening to take people around our town and to discuss what everyday life is like.

Another option is the Global Greeter Network (www.globalgreeternetwork.info). There are locals in thirty-seven countries who are willing to meet travelers and show off their city. Dan and I have not personally used this group, but travelers we know have given it great reviews. They report that greeters share not just their city but also their culture. This cultural exchange creates international friends and better understanding of a destination.

For both organizations, the guides are volunteers and meet with travelers for free. Do use safety common sense, and if for any reason you feel uncomfortable, walk away.

Stretch Your DIY Travel Dollar

Many travelers choose to do DIY trips versus tours as a way to stretch their travel dollars. This is possible, but only if you know what you are doing. We teach a class called Secrets to International Travel on a Budget (www.wildspirittravel.com), where we share our tips for reducing travel spend.

If you are planning an international honeymoon, like Dan and I did, check out The Honeymoon Hack website by Stephanie Zito (www.thehoneymoonhack.com). It is a step-by-step guide to help couples plan and take their dream honeymoon for free.

Chapter 6: Resource List

➤ Anne Berry and Angela Jacobus of Travel That Matters:
www.travelthatmatters.net

➤ Mary Cecchini of Living Big: www.livingbig.org/traveldesign

Chapter 6: Resource List (continued)

- ➤ Wild Spirit Travel—recommended travel agents: www.wildspirittravel.com/resources

- ➤ TripAdvisor travel forum: www.tripadvisor.com/forumhome

- ➤ Wild Spirit Travelers Facebook group: www.facebook.com/groups/wildspirittravelers

- ➤ Contiki tours for eighteen- to thirty-five-year-olds: www.contiki.com

- ➤ Rick Steves' Europe: www.ricksteves.com

- ➤ G Adventures: www.gadventures.com

- ➤ Wikitravel for local tour companies: www.wikitravel.org

- ➤ Wikivoyage for local tour companies: www.wikivoyage.org

- ➤ Sam's Bungalow in Bukit Lawang, Indonesia: www.samsbukitlawang.com.

- ➤ Responsible Travel: www.responsibletravel.com

- ➤ XE currency conversion: www.xe.com

- ➤ *The Volunteer Traveler's Handbook* by Shannon O'Donnell

- ➤ Volunteer Voyages: www.volunteer-voyages.com

- ➤ Wild Spirit Travel—recommended tours: www.wildspirittravel.com/resources

- ➤ Museum of New Zealand Te Papa Tongarewa: www.tepapa.govt.nz

- ➤ Eat with a Local: www.eatwithalocal.com

- ➤ Traveling Spoon: www.travelingspoon.com

- ➤ Sandemans New Europe free walking tours: www.neweuropetours.eu

- ➤ Viator: www.tourguides.viator.com

Chapter 6: Resource List (continued)

➢ Tours by Locals: www.toursbylocals.com

➢ Sevas International: www.servas.org

➢ Servas United States: www.usservas.org

➢ Global Greeter Network: www.globalgreeternetwork.info

➢ Wild Spirit Travel's Secrets to International Travel on a Budget class: www.wildspirittravel.com

➢ The Honeymoon Hack by Stephanie Zito: www.thehoneymoonhack.com

Notes: _____

_____

_____

_____

_____

_____

_____

_____

_____

_____

Notes: _____

_____

_____

_____

_____

_____

_____

_____

_____

_____

_____

_____

_____

Chapter Seven

Sleeping Around

A good night's sleep is crucial to enjoying a trip. Dan and I have stayed in lodgings ranging from hostels to five-star hotels. We enjoy discovering places locals stay when they travel as well as staying with the locals themselves. Finding unique and memorable rooms is especially fun. We have slept in lighthouses, gers, bostels (boat hostels), tree houses, and castles. This chapter covers how to find accommodations around the world.

Hotel Booking Websites

To find a good place to stay, Dan and I recommend using online websites with up-to-date reviews. A free online resource is Trip Advisor (www.tripadvisor.com). Dan and I like the fact that reviews are from average travelers, not professional guidebook writers who may get kickbacks. Unfortunately, some reviews may be biased if, for example, a competitor or a proprietor writes a review under a pseudonym. Nevertheless, most reviews are written by authentic travelers, and we find the website useful.

For reserving lodgings online, we also endorse using websites with reviews, such as Agoda (www.agoda.com), Booking.com (www.booking.com), and Hostelworld (www.hostelworld.com). Dan and I have used them around the world to find hotels, from budget to five stars. You can set filters for a particular price range or star level. The reviews are especially useful because in order to write one, you had to have booked through the website and stayed at the place.

Each booking site has slightly different payment systems. For instance, with Hostelworld, you pay a deposit to the website when you make your reservation and pay the balance to the hostel when you check in. With Agoda and Booking.com, you sometimes pay when you reserve and sometimes at the location. On a recent trip, Dan and I used all of these booking apps. Several times at check-in, we could not remember if we had already paid or not. A travel secret is to keep track of how you paid, so you don't pay twice by mistake.

There are numerous other reservation websites like these. We occasionally use others, but these are our favorites. The article "Best and Worst Hotel Booking Sites" by Reid Bramblett, on the Frommer's website (www.frommers.com/slideshows/819303-best-and-worst-hotel-booking-sites) evaluates independent booking sites as well as aggregator sites. Booking.com and Agoda are the top two in the list, which is in line with our experiences.

Unique Stays

Want to escape from cookie-cutter hotel rooms? You may find some interesting options on the websites we just mentioned, but you can also search for nontraditional accommodations on the Internet. Options are as varied as the destinations. Start by searching for what interests you and seeing if there is lodging to match. Dan and I have stayed on a pig farm in Ireland, because Dan's stepdad, Jim (a retired pig farmer), was with us. We searched for farms to find something that would interest him. That night when a sow actually gave birth, Jim was in hog heaven.

Country Tourist Offices

In many countries, you can find useful lodging information through tourist offices, also called *tourist boards* in some countries. When driving around Ireland, my sister and I stopped at a tourist board for help. Within minutes, they had us booked at a quaint bed and breakfast in Avoca, the town where *Ballykissangel* was filmed. Dan and I wanted a unique stay in France, and we were thrilled when the Bordeaux tourist office not only found us a room in a chalet on a vineyard, but arranged tours and tastings at three wineries. And we regularly used Australian tourist boards to make us reservations at pubs as we drove around that country. Many tourist boards have informative websites, but for reserving accommodations, we have found them especially useful in person.

Be warned that not all tourist offices are official. In several developing countries, tourist office signs were often just an indicator of travel agents who would get a commission if you stayed where they recommended. We rarely found these places helpful. So, be discerning on which tourist offices you use.

Good Room—Come with Me

When Dan and I started traveling, it was very common to just turn up at a bus or train station and find a group of willing home hosts offering us a good room. Sometimes the rooms were great; other times we wished we had made a reservation in advance. Still, that is how we stayed in a delightful soba (room in a private home) in Dubrovnik, Croatia, and in a tree house outside of Monteverde, Costa Rica.

The advantage of going with a willing host is you can often negotiate a reduced rate. The disadvantage is the chance of arriving and not finding anyone shouting, "Good room, come with me!" As the Internet becomes more available around the world, we have found fewer people greeting buses and trains, and instead they are listing their rooms on booking websites.

Travel Clubs

Travel clubs are a great option. Members enjoy traveling and want to meet and help other travelers. There are numerous travel clubs—

two that Dan and I are members of are Servas International and the Affordable Travel Club.

Servas International—Peace through Travel

As mentioned in chapter 6, Servas is an international travel club that promotes world peace through travel. According to the Servas website (www.servas.org), there are 15,000 members in over one hundred countries.[8] Each participating country has its own website.

Dan and I are members of Servas United States. When we travel abroad, we contact the office (www.usservas.org) and get a listing of hosts for the country we are going to. We then send email requests for home stays. If someone agrees, we stay with them *for free*. The only expectation is that we talk with them; it is a true cultural exchange. There is no requirement that we host people in return, although most members want to. We have used Servas in multiple countries and have had amazing stays every time.

One thing that differentiates Servas from other websites with free stays, where anyone can post if they have a spare bed or couch to sleep on, is that there is a vetting system. To apply for membership in Servas, you provide letters of reference and are interviewed by a local member. You also pay dues in your home country. To join, you agree to the organization's ethos of tolerance and peace through travel. We highly recommend doing some Servas stays when you travel. It was a major factor in why Dan and I were able to travel for

---

8. Servas International, accessed June 19, 2017, www.servas.org.

seven years. Not just because of the financial savings—which was nice—but it turned our trip from a sightseeing vacation to a cultural exchange where we made friends around the world.

Affordable Travel Club

The Affordable Travel Club (ATC) (www.affordabletravelclub.net) is for travelers over forty. It is based in Washington State, and while most members are in the United States, there are members around the world. We have stayed with ATC hosts in Great Britain, Spain, Australia, New Zealand, Mexico, and the United States. Americans pay yearly dues (no dues for international members), then you pay a nominal fee when you stay with someone. For example, Dan and I paid twenty US dollars to stay with an ATC host in San Francisco and thirty US dollars for a stay in Spain—affordable indeed.

As a member of ATC, it is expected that you reciprocate hosting, although there is no specific one-for-one tracking. The number of requests you receive depends on where you live. And since members are travelers, it is okay to say no to a request if you are away or simply cannot host that particular time. Dan and I often wish we would receive more requests, and most of the ATC members we have spoken to do as well.

Our ATC hosts have been a wealth of local knowledge—sharing insider travel tips and cultural information. The ATC connections we have made make the yearly dues well worth it. Full membership details are on the ATC website.

Independent Accommodations

In recent years, websites have emerged where people list their home or spare room for travelers. Some of the websites and stays are free. Others have fees or rates similar to hotels. The advantages are that these websites are easy to use and are expanding globally. The disadvantages are that there have been some bogus posts and safety issues. With all independent accommodations websites, be cautious and do your research.

Couchsurfing

The Couchsurfing website (www.couchsurfing.com) is where anyone can list a place for a traveler to stay. This may be a spare room or simply their sofa. There are no dues, and when you stay it is free. Most travelers find their stays culturally enriching and fun. But since there is no vetting process, be vigilant about your safety. Couchsurfing has a verified-member feature. It is prudent to stay with verified members that have numerous positive reviews. We strongly recommend that you read the Couchsurfing "Safety Basics" (www.couchsurfing.com/about/safety); it includes the tip that if you feel uncomfortable, leave. If you have any issues, report them to the Couchsurfing Trust and Safety Team.

Airbnb

The Airbnb website (www.airbnb.com) is where people can rent out a sofa in their living room, a spare bedroom in their house, or their entire apartment or home. The owners choose the rate, so some listings are great value, while others are the same as hotels. Still, it gives you the opportunity to see homes in different countries.

You should read all the fine print. Some listings have cleaning fees, pets living in the home, or other quirks that are best to know about before you book. Also, read the reviews. Make sure previous guests have had good stays and that people verify the photos are accurate. Keep in mind, a private room in a home may mean you are sharing the bathroom with the hosts or other guests.

On a recent trip to Central America, Dan and I used Airbnb quite a bit. When we booked, we choose private rooms and thought this would mean we would get to spend time with the local owner. However, often it was an investment property where all available rooms were rented out to travelers and the owners lived elsewhere. Since we wanted to meet locals, this was disappointing. Still, the accommodations were a great value and we had good stays.

More than once, we had problems finding the Airbnb. We learned that taxi drivers may be familiar with hotels in their city, but they didn't always know the location of Airbnb homes. Many also did not know all the street names, so having only an address did not help. Dan regularly had to turn on his smartphone and guide the taxi driver using Google Maps. Before using your smartphone overseas, take Wild Spirit Travel's Secrets to Using Technology Abroad class (www.wildspirittravel.com/courses) so you don't get hit with unexpected cell phone bills.

Rental Homes

A website Dan and I have used in a number of countries is Vacation Rental by Owner (VRBO) (www.vrbo.com). These listings are usually entire homes or apartments and may have minimum-night stay requirements. As with Airbnb, the owner sets the rate, so some are a great value, others not so much. Do read all the fine print. There are often fees for cleaning, extra people, and administration.

VRBO is part of the HomeAway family, which has a similar website (www.homeaway.com). Expedia became the parent owner to both in the spring of 2016, and this has led to some changes, especially in terms of fees. There seems to be more hidden fees, which you only discover at the final booking. Also, this buyout means VRBO is now part of a very large travel conglomerate. If you prefer to support a smaller company, try Vacasa (www.vacasa.com), based in Portland, Oregon. They don't have as many listings, but they are expanding. Dan and I have enjoyed our Vacasa stays.

House Swaps

You can also trade homes for your trip. One website for this is HomeExchange (www.homeexchange.com). Dan and I know travelers who have had amazing vacations around the world staying in someone's home, while those people stayed in theirs. The swap may include pet sitting, plant watering, or car exchange, or it may not. You discuss the details with the other homeowners and decide what is appropriate for you and them. Every swap is unique.

The travelers we know who have done this successfully suggest that you have numerous email, phone, and video conversations with the other homeowners before agreeing to swap. They also advise you to know exactly what your home and auto insurance covers before trading. There is a yearly fee to use HomeExchange; however, there is a guarantee that if you don't do a house swap in your first year, you get a second year free.

Stay Safe

Before using independent accommodations, remember that safety is more important than saving money. Read reviews. Have a backup plan. Women travelers stay with women hosts. If anything feels odd, leave. We also recommend you have a way to lock up your bags. In a person's home, you may not have a private lock on your door. Dan and I travel with padlocks to securely close our zippers, and we use a cable lock to fasten our luggage to something in the room (www.wildspirittravel.com/product/motion-detector-lock2).

Chapter 7: Resource List

- TripAdvisor: www.tripadvisor.com
- Agoda: www.agoda.com
- Booking.com: www.booking.com
- Hostelworld: www.hostelworld.com
- "Best and Worst Hotel Booking Websites" by Reid Bramblett: www.frommers.com/slideshows/819303-best-and-worst-hotel-booking-sites

Chapter 7: Resource List (continued)

- ➤ Servas International: www.servas.org
- ➤ Servas United States: www.usservas.org
- ➤ Affordable Travel Club: www.affordabletravelclub.net
- ➤ Couchsurfing: www.couchsurfing.com
- ➤ Couchsurfing safety guide: www.couchsurfing.com/about/safety
- ➤ Airbnb: www.airbnb.com
- ➤ Wild Spirit Travel's Secrets to Using Technology Abroad class: www.wildspirittravel.com/courses
- ➤ Vacation Rental by Owner: www.vrbo.com
- ➤ HomeAway: www.homeaway.com
- ➤ Vacasa: www.vacasa.com
- ➤ HomeExchange: www.homeexchange.com
- ➤ Motion-detecting cable lock: www.wildspirittravel.com/product/motion-detector-lock2

Notes: _____

_____

_____

_____

_____

_____

Notes: _____

_____

_____

_____

_____

_____

_____

_____

_____

_____

_____

_____

_____

Chapter Eight

Planes, Trains, and Camels

There are numerous forms of transport around the world. We have used planes, trains, camels, bicycles, becaks, boats, buses, sheruts, matatus, motorbikes, minivans, canoes, rickshaws, tuk-tuks, and more. Transport can be an adventure or a nightmare. Here are tips and tools to not only make reservations but to also enjoy the journey.

Planes

International flights can be the most expensive part of a trip abroad. Unfortunately, there isn't one perfect website that guarantees the cheapest flight every time to every destination. The best search engine this month may not be the best one the next time you fly. Instead of doing your research using only one website, Dan and I recommend searching on a few, as well as checking airline websites directly. The following are some of the best-known airline fare comparison websites (see the Resource List at the end of this chapter for website links):

- Expedia
- Farecompare
- Hipmunk
- Google Flights

- KAYAK
- Momondo
- Skyscanner
- Travelocity

Of these, Dan prefers Momondo, and I like Google Flights. Both are easy to use and regularly find the lowest rates. These websites also include a useful tool to set a fare alert. They monitor prices for the route and date you want, then send you a message if the price drops.

Dan and I also use the Hopper app (www.hopper.com). It is a free app on iPhones and Androids. Hopper factors in a multitude of analytics based on the best time to buy. It tells you if you should buy now or wait, then it sends you a text when you should buy. This app recently saved us 150 US dollars each on a flight to Central America.

Low-Cost Carriers

The websites mentioned in the previous section can help you find great fares on traditional airlines; however, most do not search all the low-cost, no-frills, or budget airlines. Some have started to provide rates on a few budget airlines, but not many. Momondo (www.momondo.com) is an exception, they include data on most low-cost carriers, and that is why we recommend the site.

Worldwide, there are numerous no-frills carriers that offer incredible bargain flights. For instance, in 2017, these extremely low rates were available:

- London to Milan for 13 US dollars on Ryanair
- Edinburgh to Paris for 37 US dollars on EasyJet
- Bangkok to Hanoi for 33 US dollars on AirAsia
- Delhi to Mumbai for 16 US dollars on SpiceJet[9]

Dan and I have flown on all of these, as well as SmartWings, Air Berlin, Tigerair, Jetstar Airways, and others. We found them to be comparable to economy class in traditional airlines. Sure, they may not provide a free meal or have in-flight movies, but at the discounted rate, I can buy my own food and bring a book. (See the Resource List at the end of this chapter for website links.)

Finding No-Frills Flights

The secret to finding these incredibly reduced rates is to know that no-frills airlines exist. The list of low-cost airlines on Wikipedia (en.wikipedia.org/wiki/list_of_low-cost_airlines) reveals that, at the time this book was written, there are eleven in Africa, fifty-four in Asia/Oceania, thirty-four in Europe/Middle East, and ten in South America/Latin America.

---

9. Ryanair, www.ryanair.com; EasyJet, www.easyjet.com; AirAsia, www.airasia.com; SpiceJet, www.spicejet.com, all accessed May 17, 2017.

Keeping Budget Airlines in the Budget

In order to best utilize no-frills airlines and keep them in budget, read the fine print. The low-cost airlines are infamous for nickel and diming travelers, and what they charge for varies depending on the airline and changes over time. When this book was researched, Ryanair was charging 11 to 45 US dollars to check a bag up to thirty-three pounds (depending on flight length), 2 US dollars for a standard seat (more if you want a seat with extra legroom), and 57 US dollars to check in at the airport (free to check in online.)[10] Factoring these costs in, the flight from London to Milan no longer costs 13 US dollars, but 60 US dollars as long as you can check in online when traveling, or 117 US dollars if you cannot. And if your bag is overweight, or you don't pay for it ahead of time, the fees go up quite a bit. We cover this in-depth in Secrets to International Travel on a Budget (www.wildspirittravel.com).

To keep budget flights the bargain they are meant to be, read all the rules, restrictions, and fees. Then make sure you can abide to them before buying your ticket, or you may find a wide range of surprise charges at the airport. Dan and I can travel within the regulations and save quite a bit of money by using them.

Is No-Frills No-Safe?

Wondering if no-frills airlines are safe? For the most part, their safety records are similar to other airlines. They may cut costs on in-flight

---

10. "Fees," Ryanair, accessed July 2, 2017, https://www.ryanair.com/us/en/useful-info/help-centre/fees.

food and entertainment, but most have planes comparable to traditional airlines. Unfortunately, accidents happen, and some airlines may cut corners on maintenance. If you have never heard of an airline, then research it. Dan and I have used Wizz Air in Hungary (www.wizzair.com), Nok Air in Thailand (www.nokair.com), and VivaAerobus in Mexico (www.vivaaerobus.com) just to name three that are not commonly known by American travelers. A great source of information is The West Australian Airline Ratings website (www.airlineratings.com). They provide information and safety scores on most airlines around the world.

Riding the Rails

Traveling by train can be a great way to get around. Instead of quickly flying over a country, you leisurely meander through the countryside, talking to locals and seeing real life. At least, that is the romantic view of train travel. Sometimes, it is a nice, relaxed way to experience a country. Other times, you are packed in like sardines and cruising at over 200 miles per hour.

The fastest train Dan and I have been on was in China. The Shanghai Maglev goes from the city to the airport, and for a few brief moments reaches 430 kilometers per hour (or 267 miles per hour). Fast and fun, so worth doing at least once. But we have had other train journeys we would like to forget. We had a rat in our train car on a trip in India. There was a window missing on an overnight train in Thailand, which meant the trip was freezing cold. We have been in standing-room-only trains throughout Asia and Europe. We spent thirty-six hours on the Trans-Siberian railroad (about ten hours longer than predicted due to many delays), packed into a train car with no showers. Yes, not every train trip is *romantic*.

Nevertheless, Dan and I still enjoy taking the train and do recommend it. It is a cultural experience. And some can be luxurious, such as the Orient Express. For information on scenic trips, read "World's 15 Most Scenic Train Rides" by Donna Heiderstadt, on the Fodor's Travel website (www.fodors.com/news/photos/worlds-15-most-scenic-train-rides).

The Man in Seat 61

To find out what a train is like before you take it, go to The Man in Seat 61 website (www.seat61.com). This site has a wealth of information on everything a traveler needs to know about a train. It not only says whether it is comfortable—although that is covered—but it also has schedules, pricing, how to buy tickets, what stations and train cars are like, tips for which class of ticket to buy, which side of the train to sit on, and the information goes on and on. It is not just written data but also has photos, whenever possible, so you can actually see what the seats or the toilets are like. It really is amazing. When Dan and I were in foreign lands, this website was sometimes our only source of information in English on train times.

Wandering with a Railpass

When Dan first traveled to Europe in the 1980s, the Eurail pass was the way to go. However, it is no longer the bargain it once was. If you are wondering if you should get a railpass when wandering around Europe, read "Eurail or InterRail" on The Man in Seat 61 website (www.seat61.com/railpass-and-eurail-pass-guide.htm). It is the most comprehensive guide on this topic that Dan and I have discovered.

Sleeper Trains

Taking an overnight train can save time, because it lets you get to your next destination without wasting a day. That is, as long as you can sleep on the train. If the train is uncomfortable or noisy and you can't sleep, you may find that you spend your first day at the new destination catching up on sleep instead of seeing sights. The quality of sleeper trains varies greatly around the world. Plus, you need to know the difference between classes when buying your ticket. For instance, in India there are eight classes: AC-1, AC 2-tier, AC 3-tier, first class, AC executive chair, AC chair, sleeper class, and second class. Dan and I liked AC 2-tier best. It is hard to know what class you will be comfortable in, unless you do your research on The Man in Seat 61 website.

Securing Your Stuff when Sleeping

You'll want to make sure your bags are safe on a sleeper train. No matter how comfortable the train car, Dan nor I would sleep well if our bags were stowed where anyone could walk off with them during the night. That is why we lock our bags to something (usually a post, our seat, or a luggage rack) using cable locks whenever we are on a train, bus, or boat. The cable lock we use is available on our website (www.wildspirittravel.com/product/motion-detector-lock2). It has a motion detector that we set when in hotels, but we do not turn it on when on moving transport.

Bumpy Buses

Unfortunately, there is no website like The Man in Seat 61 for buses around the world. As with trains, Dan and I have had some great bus journeys and also have discovered ones we would not take again. In general, we prefer flying or traveling by train in Europe, Australia, Asia, and North America. In New Zealand, the buses are clean and efficient, and luckily, you never have to be on them too long because every few hours there is something worth getting off to see. In Africa, there are not many choices, so we stuck with buses—even though they can be harrowing uncomfortable journeys.

Buses are our transport of choice in South America and Central America. We found long-distance day buses—often called *chicken buses* since locals carry anything and everything on board, including chickens—to be a fun cultural experience. Sure, they might be bumpy, cramped, and a bit crazy, but that is the joy. Also, in that region of the world, night buses can be delightful, especially if you go first or luxury class. These high-end options may only be a few dollars more than regular buses but way more comfortable—envision leather recliners at eighty miles per hour. In Argentina, Dan and I did a first-class night bus where the seats turned into flat beds, there were movies with English subtitles, and we were served a hot dinner with champagne. Yes, champagne on a bus. Now that is enjoyable, and definitely a bus journey Dan and I would take again.

Sailing the Seas

Boat journeys can be a pleasant way to travel abroad. From canoes to catamarans to ferries of all sizes, there are many options. In numerous countries, you just head to the water and see what ship is there that will take you to your destination.

The best resource for ferry information is the AFerry.com website (www.aferry.com). You can book tickets for over twelve hundred ferry routes in Europe. Although not nearly as extensive in the rest of the world, they do have some ferry information in Asia, Africa, North America, South America, and Oceania.

If you are thinking of taking a cruise, do some research. They vary in terms of quality, cost, and care. Travel agents are a good option to consult with about cruise ships. An online source is Cruise Critic (www.cruisecritic.com).

Boats that Float

On all boats, make sure the vessel seems safe and is not overcrowded. In some parts of the world, there are no rules or regulations for boat operators. We have seen many boats dangerously overcrowded and heading off in rough seas. Be responsible for your own safety.

Before doing water activities in developing countries, ask about safety options. When we were in Laos, Dan went to float on the river in Vang Vieng. The company renting inner tubes was out of life jackets, so Dan did not go. He went the next day, wearing a life jacket, and had a great time. We later found out that a traveler drowned that week inner tubing without a life vest.

Driving Overseas

Driving in a foreign country is something to study before you do. Renting a car gives you independence; however, it can be confusing, dangerous, and a hassle. In big cities around the world, a car is often not needed because public transport is readily available and easy to use. In some countries, streets are in poor condition, plus there may not be signs or lights. Road rules differ around the world, and in some areas, are nonexistent. If you do not know how the locals drive, you will be a hazard.

International Road Rules

If you are thinking of driving on an international trip, find out what side of the road they drive on and the customary speed limits. AAA and international rental car agencies may be able to provide a guide on driving in a foreign destination. Also, study road signs used in the country. On the Wikipedia website (www.wikipedia.org), you can type in the search field "road signs in" plus the country you are visiting to see the signs used in specific countries. Wikipedia also has a useful chart comparing all of the European road signs (en.wikipedia.org/wiki/comparison_of_European_road_signs).

Rental Car Companies

There are several international rental car companies, such as Hertz, Budget, or Alamo. If you have a favorite agency, then see if they service your destination. A number of the fare websites mentioned at the start of this chapter, including Expedia, Hipmunk, and Momondo, give car-rental quotes, too. Also, read "Tips for Booking a Rental Car" by Rick Steves, on the Rick Steves' Europe website (www.ricksteves.com/travel-tips/transportation/booking-a-car). In this article, he recommends renting from a consolidator like Auto Europe (www.autoeurope.com). Do not let the name fool you; this website works worldwide.

Dan and I found it was sometimes cheaper and easier to rent a car from a small local company when abroad. Often, these agencies do not show up in search engines. A good source for finding small rental car companies is the DriverAbroad.com website (www.driverabroad.com). It also has general advice for self-driving in over two hundred countries, islands, or territories.

Rental Car Restrictions

Many international rental car agencies have age restrictions. For drivers under twenty-five, options may be limited or there may be additional fees. On the other end of the spectrum, some rental car companies will not lend a car to someone seventy and over, and if they do, they may require proof of good driving and of good health. Yup, you may need to have a doctor's note to rent a car—something you would definitely need to get before you go. For information on renting a car in Europe, read "Rental-Car Red Tape in Europe" by Rick Steves (www.ricksteves.com/travel-tips/transportation/rental-car-requirements). For information on other destinations, do an Internet search or check the policies of international agencies (such as Hertz or Avis) to see what they require.

International Car Insurance

When you rent a car, the agency may require insurance. Getting insurance from the agency may cost more than the daily rental fee. However, insurance is important. Take time to consider your insurance options before you are at the counter picking up the keys. Most US auto policies do not cover international rental cars, but it never hurts to ask. If you pay for a rental with a credit card, there may be insurance through the card. If they do offer insurance, there may be rules, such as you have to turn down the rental agency's insurance to have coverage.

If you are a member of a motoring club, such as AAA, check if there are affiliate clubs where you are going. Having emergency roadside coverage abroad can be handy. Dan and I were happy to have our AAA membership when our car would not start at a train station in France. Also, when you rent a car, take photos from every angle. This will help prove that a dent was already on the car before you rented it.

International Driving Permit

An international driving permit (IDP) is a translation of your driver's license in eleven languages. Alone, it is not proof that you are eligible to drive. You still need to carry your driver's license. In the United States, you can get an IDP at AAA (AAA membership is not required). It is valid for one year.

Not every country, or every rental agency, requires international drivers to have an IDP. If you know you are going to rent a car abroad, check with agencies at your destination. DriverAbroad.com lists countries that require an IDP (www.driverabroad.com/self-drive/international-driving-permit).

Do not forget to take your real driver's license. Even if you are not planning to drive in a foreign country, Dan and I recommend traveling with your license, just in case. When we were in Thailand, Dan decided to do a Thai massage course in Chiang Mai for two weeks. I decided to explore on my own and took a bus to a town called Pai. Neither Dan nor I planned to drive in Thailand. However, in Pai, I got very sick and ended up in a hospital. Luckily, Dan had his driver's license so he could rent a car and come get me. Sometimes plans change or there are emergencies. Having a license and an IDP gives you flexibility.

Motoring on a Motorbike

In some countries, motorbikes are common, and renting them is easy—you may not even need a driver's license. Motoring around on a motorbike can be fun. However, be safe about it. Wear a helmet and closed-toed shoes, and only rent a motorbike if you know how to drive one. Just because an agency will rent to anyone, does not make it safe. Dan and I met numerous travelers with scars from being in motorbike accidents. Many of them had never driven one before, but when they found out that didn't matter, they went for it. I had never driven a motorbike before traveling internationally, and still have not. Overseas is not the place to learn. If you think driving a motorbike sounds fun, learn how before you go abroad.

Other Ways to Traverse the Globe

There are many other ways to get from point A to point B on an international trip. Explore unique transport options at your destination. *Matatus* in Kenya are hot, crowded minivans that can be a heck of a lot of fun. *Becaks* (cycle rickshaws) in Indonesia are a beloved way to get around, and even though they have been banned several times in some cities for causing traffic jams, they still remain. Animal power is the way to go in Tunisia. Crossing the Sahara by camel is a travel experience Dan and I will never forget.

Remember, it is often the journey, rather than the destination, that is the most memorable.

Chapter 8: Resource List

➤ Expedia: www.expedia.com/flights
➤ Farecompare: www.farecompare.com
➤ Hipmunk: www.hipmunk.com
➤ Google Flights: www.google.com/flights

Chapter 8: Resource List (continued)

- ➢ KAYAK: www.kayak.com

- ➢ Momondo: www.momondo.com

- ➢ Skyscanner: www.skyscanner.com

- ➢ Travelocity: www.travelocity.com

- ➢ Hopper: www.hopper.com

- ➢ Ryanair: www.ryanair.com

- ➢ EasyJet: www.easyjet.com

- ➢ AirAsia: www.airasia.com

- ➢ SpiceJet: www.spicejet.com

- ➢ SmartWings: www.smartwings.com/en

- ➢ Air Berlin: www.airberlin.com

- ➢ Tigerair: www.tigerair.com

- ➢ JetStar Airways: www.jetstar.com

- ➢ List of low-cost airlines on Wikipedia: en.wikipedia.org/wiki/list_of_low-cost_airlines

- ➢ Wild Spirit Travel's Secrets to International Travel on a Budget class: www.wildspirittravel.com

- ➢ Wizz Air: www.wizzair.com

- ➢ Nok Air: www.nokair.com

- ➢ VivaAerobus: www.vivaaerobus.com/en

- ➢ The West Australian Airline Ratings: www.airlineratings.com

- ➢ "World's 15 Most Scenic Train Rides" by Donna Heiderstadt (May 8, 2015): www.fodors.com/news/photos/worlds-15-most-scenic-train-rides

- ➢ The Man in Seat 61: www.seat61.com

Chapter 8: Resource List (continued)

- ➤ "Eurail or InterRail": www.seat61.com/railpass-and-eurail-pass-guide.htm

- ➤ Motion-detecting cable lock: www.wildspirittravel.com/product/motion-detector-lock2

- ➤ AFerry.com: www.aferry.com

- ➤ Cruise Critic: www.cruisecritic.com

- ➤ International road signs: www.wikipedia.org

- ➤ European road signs: en.wikipedia.org/wiki/comparison_of_European_road_signs

- ➤ "Tips for Booking a Rental Car" by Rick Steves: www.ricksteves.com/travel-tips/transportation/booking-a-car

- ➤ Auto Europe: www.autoeurope.com

- ➤ DriverAbroad.com: www.driverabroad.com

- ➤ "Rental-Car Red Tape in Europe" by Rick Steves: www.ricksteves.com/travel-tips/transportation/rental-car-requirements

- ➤ Information on international driving permits: www.driverabroad.com/self-drive/international-driving-permit

Notes: _____

_____

_____

_____

_____

Notes: _____

_____

_____

_____

_____

_____

_____

_____

_____

_____

_____

_____

_____

_____

Chapter Nine

Returning Home

There comes a time when your trip is over and you have to return home. Sorry to make you think about this before you even go, but it is good to plan ahead for the end of an international trip. This chapter gives resources for American travelers. Many countries have similar websites for their citizens—international readers should research the rules, limits, and regulations for their country.

Thinking about the End before It Has Begun

Dan and I recommend getting to your departure city at least a day in advance. For instance, if your flight home is on the fourth, get to the city on the third. You don't want to miss an international flight because there is a transport delay or road closure. Plan to arrive in advance so you can deal with *what-if* situations.

Packing It In

Before your trip, consider your flight home. Most airlines have restrictive rules about checked baggage and carry-ons. When Dan and I first traveled, we could show up for our return flight with extra bags from all of our shopping. More than once, I waddled down the plane aisle with three or four large shopping bags filled with souvenirs, in addition to my carry-on.

Now, having extra bags is an issue. If you go on a shopping spree while abroad, you may have to pay heavy fees to get your goodies home. Have a plan if you are going to shop. A tip my mom gave me when I first started traveling was to take some old clothes. Then on the last days of the trip, throw them out to make room in your suitcase for souvenirs.

US Customs

If you do shop, be aware of the rules at the US Customs and Border Protection (CBP) (www.cbp.gov). There are duty free limits and restrictions on what you can bring home. These change over time and vary based on countries, so check before each trip. If you spend more than the duty-free allowance, you will have to pay taxes on the overage. And some items have special limits, such as alcohol and tobacco. For more information on this topic, read "Returning Home: Going through US Customs" by Shyla Esko Bare, on the Wild Spirit Travel website (www.wildspirittravel.com/returninghome).

When shopping abroad, keep track of the money you spend. This is especially important if you negotiate a great deal on an item. For instance, if there is a thousand-US dollar piece of art you have bargained down to seven hundred US dollars, get a receipt. Otherwise, CBP may think it is over the duty-free limit, and you will owe taxes. This also helps with the declaration form travelers complete upon entering the United States (www.cbp.gov/travel/us-citizens/sample-declaration-form).

The form is going digital, so I find it especially important to be familiar with it before traveling. In the past, it would be handed out on the flight—providing plenty of time to contemplate the questions and fill it out completely. However, at many airports it is now done at computer kiosks once you have landed. That means there may be a long line of passengers waiting to get to the machine. When this happens, I feel flustered and rushed, so it helps that I am already familiar with the form.

Food—Fine or Fineable?
You will want to verify current rules on bringing food home. Often, travelers can bring in packaged food like cookies and chips. Even some cheeses and fish are allowed. However, travelers may be fined for bringing in fruits, vegetables, and some meat products. You will need to declare all food items you bring back. To avoid hassles and having food confiscated at customs, check the Don't Pack a Pest website (www.dontpackapest.com/travel-guidelines) for lists of allowed and banned food and agricultural products.

Trusted Traveler Programs

There are several programs that enable travelers to be *preapproved* for travel. These include TSA Pre✓®, Global Entry, Nexus, and Sentri. Nexus is for people who frequently cross the Canadian–United States border, while Sentri is for the Mexican border. TSA Pre✓ and Global Entry have wider scopes, so we will focus on these.

TSA Pre✓

The Transportation Security Administration (TSA) is a branch of the US Department of Homeland Security. TSA employees screen air travelers. The days of showing up for a flight just before takeoff are gone. Now, depending on the airport, the security lines can be lengthy, requiring passengers to arrive well in advance of a flight. Plus, there is the fun of taking off shoes, removing electronic devices from bags, and so forth.

TSA Pre✓ (www.tsa.gov/precheck) lets passengers go through a special line that is normally faster and does not require removal of shoes, liquids, or laptops. According to the TSA website, in May 2017, the security line was less than a five-minute wait for 97% of travelers with TSA Pre✓. Getting into the program involves an application, a background check, an interview, and fingerprinting. It costs 85 US dollars for a five-year membership.[11]

But before you sign up and pay the fee, you may want to consider the Global Entry plan instead. TSA Pre✓ gets you in the

---

11. TSA Pre✓, accessed June 19, 2017, http://www.tsa.gov/precheck.

fast line leaving a US airport, but Global Entry works both ways. It includes the TSA Pre✓ as well as an expedited return. If you get the TSA Pre✓ first, you cannot *upgrade* to Global Entry; you have to apply separately and pay the entire Global Entry fee.

Global Entry
Global Entry is through US Customs and Border Protection (www.cbp.gov/travel/trusted-traveler-programs/global-entry). It is a program that gives *low-risk travelers* expedited clearance when returning to the United States. That means they get to skip the long lines at immigration when flying home from a trip.

Getting on this fast track costs minimally more than TSA Pre✓, which is included in Global Entry. To qualify, you must apply, pass an extensive background check, and have an in-person interview. The fee is nonrefundable and the process can take months, as many travelers apply for Global Entry. Still, if you are a regular international traveler with a clean background, this program may be a good option.

Chapter 9: Resource List

- ➢ US Customs and Border Protection: www.cbp.gov
- ➢ "Returning Home: Going through US Customs" by Shyla Esko Bare (July 27, 2017): www.wildspirittravel.com/returninghome
- ➢ US Customs and Border Protection Customs Declaration Form: www.cbp.gov/travel/us-citizens/sample-declaration-form

Chapter 9: Resource List (continued)

➤ Don't Pack a Pest: www.dontpackapest.com/travel-guidelines

➤ Transportation Security Administration Pre✓: www.tsa.gov/precheck

➤ US Customs and Border Protection Global Entry: www.cbp.gov/travel/trusted-traveler-programs/global-entry

Notes: _____

_____

_____

_____

_____

_____

_____

_____

_____

_____

Notes: _____

_____

_____

_____

_____

_____

_____

_____

_____

_____

_____

_____

_____

Chapter Ten

Have Fun!

Dan and I have saved our most important travel tip for last. That is *have fun*! International travel should be enjoyable. The reason we continued traveling around the world for seven years is because we were having an incredible time. Our trip was filled with laughter, enlightenment, and luxurious moments that left us wanting to travel more and more. Sure, sometimes we had troubles and issues, but those lessened as we traveled and discovered the secrets presented in this book.

This is the first book in the Travel Smart Strategies series. Many other tips and tools—such as packing, using technology abroad, budget travel, and safety—are covered extensively in other books and classes within this series. Visit (www.wildspirittravel.com) for our entire range of travel topics.

All the resources, insights, and travel secrets in this book were presented with one goal in mind: to enable travelers, like you, to have an amazing international trip. Once you have a specific destination in mind, we encourage you to get inspired about that country. Before you go, immerse yourself in the culture. Read a book that is based in the area. Watch movies filmed there. Delve in before your flight, so the preparation will feel exciting. This is just one of many to-dos you will find on Wild Spirit Travel's Travel Planning Checklist (www.wildspirittravel.com/book-checklist).

If you still have questions, join the Wild Spirit Travelers Facebook group (www.facebook.com/groups/wildspirittravelers). Members include travelers from around the world. Dan and I moderate this group and answer what we can, plus other travelers chime in as well. Even if you don't have questions, join so you can share your insights with others. It is also a great place to post a photo or two from your international travels to inspire travel dreamers to journey abroad. Happy Travels!

Chapter 10: Resource List

➢ Wild Spirit Travel: www.wildspirittravel.com

➢ Wild Spirit Travel's Travel Planning Checklist: www.wildspirittravel.com/book-checklist

➢ Wild Spirit Travelers Facebook group: www.facebook.com/groups/wildspirittravelers

Notes: _____

_____

_____

_____

_____

_____

_____

_____

_____

_____

_____

_____

_____

_____

Index

Wild Spirit Travel Classes
Taught at Colleges, Clubs, and Other Venues

International Travel Secrets Revealed Series

- International Travel Prep: Before You Go Abroad
- Secrets to International Travel on a Budget
- Secrets to Solo Travel Abroad
- Secrets to Using Technology Abroad
- The Art of Packing for an International Trip
- Women's Travel Secrets Revealed

DIY Travel Series

- Australia for Travelers
- Great Britain for Travelers
- Ireland for Travelers
- SE Asia for Travelers
- Central America for Travelers
- India for Travelers
- Mexico for Travelers
- Western Europe for Travelers

Travel Secrets for Travelers over 50

- Travel Smart Workshop
- Essential Tools Workshop

Other Classes

- Travel Smarter, Safer, Cheaper (three-class series)
- Point-n-Shoot Travel Photography

Wild Spirit Travel Digital Classes

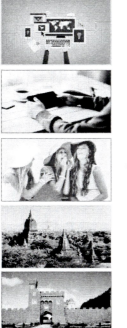

International Travel Prep: Before You Go

Secrets to Using Technology Abroad

Women's Travel Secrets Revealed

SE Asia for Travelers: Essential Tips & Tools

Ireland for Travelers

Digital classes are available online as a video course optimized for smartphones, tablets, and computers that you can access anytime anywhere (www.wildspirittravel.com/courses). Classes are also available on thumb drives (www.wildspirittravel.com/shop), perfect to watch on PCs or Macs. All courses are two-and-a-half hours, divided into nine to twelve lessons, so you can watch all at once or as you wish. Each one also comes with a comprehensive handout.

Connect with Us:

 Wild Spirit Travel Facebook Page

 Wild Spirit Travelers Facebook Group

 Wild_Spirit_Traveler Instagram Photos

 Wild Spirit Traveler Pinterest Boards

 @WildSpiritTrvlr Twitter Handle

Wild Spirit Travel YouTube Channel

Let us know when you are traveling by using our hashtags:

#WildSpiritTravel

#TravelSmartStrategies

#TSS-B4UGo

Please Review This Book on Amazon.com

One of the best ways you can help us get more exposure for our book is to write an honest and thoughtful review. If you liked this book, please take a moment to find our book on Amazon.com and find the Write a Customer Review button. Thank you.

About the Authors

Before traveling around the world, Dan Bare racked up frequent-flyer points working as a computer consultant across the United States, Canada, and the United Kingdom. Thus far, he has visited seventy-four countries and forty-seven states. Dan has a master diploma of business from Central Queensland University in Australia.

In her teens, Shyla Esko Bare set a goal of visiting over one hundred countries. Her first solo international trip was at twenty-one when she backpacked across Australia. Shyla has been to seventy-three countries and counting. She has a bachelor of arts in business from the University of Washington and a master of business administration from Edinburgh Napier University in Scotland.

Together, they have lived in Scotland, Australia, Thailand, and Mexico and have traveled around the world, visiting countries on six continents. Dan and Shyla are global citizens who currently reside

near Portland, Oregon, when they are not traversing the globe. They are founders of Wild Spirit Travel and producers of the Travel Smart Strategies series of books, classes, and YouTube travel tips. Dan and Shyla are also keynote travel presenters who have delighted audiences on three continents.